The World Recast

Winnetka-Northfield Public Library

3 1240 00582 2916

DEC - 2017

WITHDRAWN

D1608441

WINNETKA-NORTHFIELD
PUBLIC LIBRARY DISTRICT
WINNETKA, IL 60093
847-446-7220

The World Recast

70 Buildings from 70 Years of *Concrete Quarterly*

Nick Jones

Introduction

1947–1959

1960–1969

1970–1979

1980–1989

1990–1999

2000–2009

2010–2017

Featured Issues

A Short History of *Concrete Quarterly*

Image Credits

Acknowledgements

Introduction
Hugh Pearman

"I don't care about your church, I didn't ask you to do it. And if I do it, I'll do it my way. It interests me because it's a plastic work. It's difficult." This from the man who wrote the book on architectural arrogance, Le Corbusier, to his Dominican priest-artist-client Marie-Alain Couturier. The letter concerned the 1955 pilgrimage church of Notre Dame du Haut at Ronchamp in eastern France, one of the greatest works of post-war architecture. No, Corb didn't do God. But he could do—what? The numinous? If you go there, you'll understand. And so did Couturier, who also commissioned Le Corbusier for the monastery of Sainte Marie de La Tourette near Lyon that you will find in this book—and having done so, died before either of these buildings was finished.

"A plastic work". At first this might seem an odd way to describe working in concrete, but of course Corb was using the word in its correct sense. Concrete is mouldable to virtually any shape you want, though great skill is needed in the construction of the moulds. It has to be carefully crafted. Beyond that, it can be rapidly built. It can be both structure and surface. It can be coloured, tiled or left self-finished. Even in its raw state it comes in a myriad of colours and textures depending on its composition, from smooth blinding white through nubbly honey-coloured pebble-rich mixes to dark industrial greys.

Small wonder, then, that concrete is one of the prime materials of modernist architecture and design-led engineering, almost a manifesto product—one that Corb did much to popularise. It suited the narrative of modernism both aesthetically and technologically, but it also allowed a sculptural, tactile element that is hard to obtain, say, in a steel-frame, glazed-curtain-wall building. In that respect it has more in common with traditional masonry finishes. But whereas the only way brick can span thin air is by means of arches or domes of various kinds, reinforced concrete allows a different approach with wider spans—if you want that. In a bridge, you certainly do. In a building, not necessarily. When is a flat beam or slab more than just prosaic? When, say, the exaltation of the beam and slab becomes almost the entire architecture, as at Denys Lasdun's 1960s–1970s National Theatre in London. Or when that simplest of construction techniques, post-and-beam, becomes glorified, even fetishised, in a project such as London's Barbican with its sense of colossal mass.

The buildings in this book, ranging around the world, show the diversity of uses and forms possible. What links Jørn Utzon's 1950s–1970s Sydney Opera House, say, with Zaha Hadid's 2004 Phaeno Science Centre in Wolfsburg, Germany? Not appearance, for sure. Virtuosity, certainly. But also the way they challenged the possible, in particular the computing power available at the time to their engineers, in both cases strained to the utmost. Those two buildings marked significant advances in structural knowledge, as had an earlier generation of architects and engineers working with thin-shell concrete, such as that found in the 1940s Brynmawr Rubber Factory by Architects Co-Partnership with engineers Ove Arup and Partners.

New and evolving technology in pursuit of ever more audacious 'plastic' forms is only part of the story however. There is the parallel story of the concrete component, the factory-made part for dry assembly. Here you could look at another pair of buildings: the 1970 Combination Room at Cambridge's Downing College by architects Howell Killick Partridge & Amis (HKPA), and the 2015 Stirling Prize-winning Burntwood School in south-west London by Allford Hall Monaghan Morris. These represent what HKPA's Bill Howell called "vertebrate architecture", calling to mind boniness and—very important—articulation. Seeing the joints is as important to that kind of architecture as the monolithic appearance is to moulded, 'plastic' concrete buildings.

You might well want to expose your expensively crafted concrete, be it rough in the brutalist manner or silky smooth in the Japanese way. Dublin's Grafton Architects are to the fore on this, as with their 2009 Bocconi University in Milan. But you might not want to see or feel it at all. You might want it to do its job less overtly, be overlaid or mixed with other materials, as at Sir Basil Spence's 1960s Sussex University where concrete and brick co-exist—a trick he picked up from Le Corbusier's later work. Beyond that, plenty of famous buildings don't shout their concrete-ness but they are concrete, under the skin. It's not the first thing you think of with Frank Lloyd Wright's

One that got away... *Concrete Quarterly* never visited Le Corbusier's legendary church of Notre Dame du Haut at Ronchamp, France, but it did publish this photograph in autumn 1965.

THE WORLD RECAST: 70 BUILDINGS FROM 70 YEARS OF *CONCRETE QUARTERLY*

1951 Johnson Wax building in Illinois, or Stanton Williams' 2010 Stirling Prize-winning Sainsbury Laboratory in Cambridge.

Nor do you associate it with British High Tech, which appears to be all about assembling steel, aluminium and glass components in various eye-catching ways. But Richard Rogers' Lloyd's of London building is concrete, and Nicholas Grimshaw's Waterloo International rail terminal is a hybrid layer-cake—steel and glass for the top layer, concrete (well made, proudly exposed) for the levels below the tracks. This hybrid configuration is shared by the newest building in this book, Renzo Piano Building Workshop's Stavros Niarchos Foundation Cultural Centre in Athens. A planted, landscape concrete acropolis culminating in a delicate High Tech Parthenon, you might say. That beautiful roof is itself a hybrid of smooth ferrocement around a steel-frame armature: an exemplary aesthetic resulting from advanced (and earthquake-resistant) technology.

Certain places, certain architects, are defined by the material—Oscar Niemeyer's Brazilian buildings for instance, or Félix Candela's in Mexico.

It's a great leveller, allowing less advanced economies to compete with more technologically advanced ones. Everyone knows how to make the stuff, it's what you then choose to do with it that counts. The result is often lyrical, an expression of joy in the skilful manipulation of a near-universal material.

Universal? Indeed: you will find it in some sensitive historic contexts, used sometimes unexpectedly. One of my personal favourites is in Llandaff Cathedral in Cardiff. It had been badly war-damaged, and the young architect George Pace was entrusted with its restoration in 1949. As well as restoring, he added: most notably the astonishingly bold 'pulpitum', dividing the nave in half rather like the ancient rood screen did—but which instead bestrides the nave like some holy robot carrying part of the organ and an aluminium sculpture by Jacob Epstein. It makes this little cathedral unique and has more impact than many sizeable buildings. Refined, somehow unearthly—we're back at Ronchamp with Corb and his difficult 'plastic' works. You sense the excitement of those times, continuing today: anything was, and is, possible.

Royal Festival Hall
London, UK
Robert Matthew, Peter Moro, Leslie Martin
Issue 12, Autumn 1951

With peace came concrete. After 1945, swathes of Europe faced reconstruction on an unprecedented scale. In Britain more than 450,000 houses had been destroyed or rendered uninhabitable by bombing raids. But at the same time, as architect Hugh Casson would remember 40 years later, the whole country was "warmed by a belief that this time round things could and would be better".[1] It was a period of relentless activity as architects and engineers led the charge into the future, designing schools, hospitals, factories, new towns, entirely new ways of living. People would travel by motorways, some would live in towers, all would have access to electricity and decent sanitation. There would be new power plants, sewage works, state-of-the-art collieries.

This was the modern world rising expectantly from the rubble in 1947. This was the world that Concrete Quarterly was founded to record.

Concrete was the obvious material with which to shape this world. While timber and steel were both under ration, concrete was cheap and relatively plentiful. It was reassuringly familiar, having been used as a structural material in Britain for over half a century. (Despite the general spirit of optimism, there was an understandable battle-weariness towards novelty—

"Invention and elaboration and discovery are no longer friends on whom we can rely", wrote Concrete Quarterly in 1951, "and even Progress—half Goddess, half Victorian matron—is not necessarily on the side of the angels."[2])

But concrete was also undeniably modern and had benefited from the single-minded inventiveness of wartime. Prestressed concrete, for example, had not been used in the UK until it had been called upon to replace steel in the roof beams of underground munitions stores, and timber in the railway sleepers needed to keep troop cars rolling. By the late 1940s, the technique had transformed the construction of factories and warehouses, as well as the long-span bridges that made the new motorways feasible.

Builders such as Wimpey and Wates were also putting their war experience to new uses. Wates had built runways, ordnance factories, military camps and, most famously, the concrete pontoons for the Mulberry harbours at the D-Day landing beaches. It was now using the techniques of factory building and mechanised lifting to build permanent housing quickly and without the need for skilled labour (of which there was a desperate shortage). "Not many years ago the idea of factory-made houses was considered as a dream of the future, suitable only for books like HG Wells' *Shape of Things to Come*", wrote *Concrete Quarterly* in 1948.[3] Now it was a reality, and one on which many thousands of families depended.

In aesthetics too, concrete was a material whose time had come. *Concrete Quarterly* may have occasionally got carried away in its estimation of concrete's capacity for beauty ("Crawley industrial district is— yes—charming"), but in an age of privation, where any excess could be viewed as morally questionable, there was something inherently appealing about a material that could be both structure and finish.[4] Efficiency of form had long been a maxim of modernist architecture, but never had it chimed so strongly with the public mood. Even at the Festival of Britain's celebratory, fairground-like South Bank Exhibition, the visual appeal of many of the buildings lay in the shape of their bones.

As a result, the 1950s saw the emergence of a new type of visionary building designer—not an architect, but an architect-engineer who could distil a building into its inherent structural form and create something awe-inspiring. Félix Candela in Mexico used the same technique of creating impossibly thin concrete shells to build both warehouses and cathedrals. Pier Luigi Nervi in Italy built beautiful stadiums, skyscrapers and auditoriums that were simply "physical materialization of the play of forces at work within them".[5] Ove Arup in Britain could build a rubber factory that was also a "floating ship of luminosity in space and sky".[6] All three men were described in terms associated with art as much as science. Nervi's structural theories, for example, added up to "in effect, the importance of *feeling* for material, and an intuitive perception of its capabilities—a perception in which calculations are of value only as corroboration".[7]

There were paradoxes at play in post-war architecture and engineering. On the one hand, this was an age in which science and research were taking a more prominent role, both in the construction industry, and in society generally—"Any bus-top conversation splits the atom", noted editor Betty Campbell in 1949.[8] But on the other, as understanding of concrete and its structural properties increased, the nature of its visual power was becoming more mysterious. Perhaps it was simply that, as Nervi had it, "concrete was a living creature".[9]

Hams Hall Power Station
Birmingham, UK
Richard Alexander Chattock,
LG Mouchel and Partners

Issue 4, Winter 1948

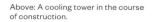
Above: A cooling tower in the course
of construction.

Right: The second phase of the works
was nearing completion in the winter
of 1948. The first phase had been
constructed during the war.

The four cooling towers were reputed to be the largest in the world. Each had a capacity of 4 million gallons an hour.

In 1947 and 1948, the early issues of *Concrete Quarterly* were focused on one thing above all else: power. There simply wasn't enough. "Full employment, a favourable trade balance, more goods in the shops, the re-equipment of industry, a restored European economy and an increased influence for Britain" all depended on an increase in energy production, chiefly, but not entirely, through the burning of coal.[10] By the end of 1948, the first four issues had reported on two modernised collieries, three hydroelectric dams and four power stations.

Of these, Hams Hall B Station in Birmingham was easily the most imposing, standing as it did on the outskirts of England's second city. The hyperbolic cooling tower was probably the most iconic concrete form of the twentieth century and the four here were at the time the largest in the world: each as tall as Giles Gilbert Scott's mighty Liverpool Cathedral and with the capacity to cool 4 million gallons of water an hour. With steel reinforcement for concrete still under rationing, this was a staggering endeavour. But then, as *Concrete Quarterly* pointed out, "Birmingham... has always done things in a big way." Throughout the 1950s, it would be "one of the foremost cities in Europe in [its] range of redevelopment", with one of Britain's first multilevel shopping centres, a trailblazing inner ring road and a hugely expanded university among its achievements.[11]

The numbers involved in the construction of Hams Hall must have made astonishing reading in austerity-stricken post-war Britain. It was designed to produce 300,000 kilowatts of electrical power, for which it needed up to 8,000 tonnes of coal a day. *Concrete Quarterly* could not help but compare this with the "meagre allocation" of the rationed British family and wonder how long it would take them to burn "the same amount as this monster will consume daily". Another "sobering thought in this mass of giant figures" was the cost of the station: estimated to be £10.5 million today. "Perhaps you find these figures too mighty for meaning?" wondered *Concrete Quarterly*. "Then try it this way! A man earning £500 a year would have to have started working nearly 20,000 years before the beginning of the Christian era to earn that amount. Does that make it easier?"

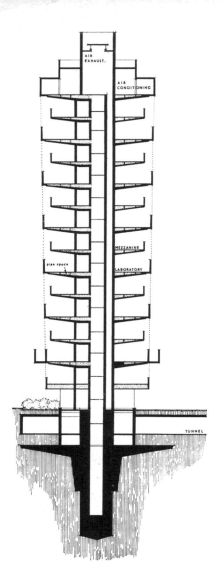

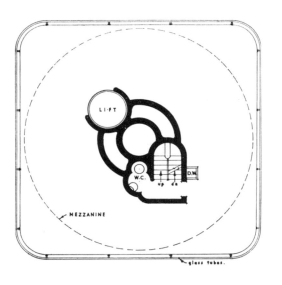

Johnson Wax Research Tower
Racine, Wisconsin, US
Frank Lloyd Wright

Issue 10, Spring 1951

Above: Section through the tower, with its structure of trunk, branches and root.

Above right: Plan showing the central core.

Right: The structure awaiting its glass skin.

Below: Board sheeting entirely enclosed the building during construction, making it possible to work throughout the winter.

Right: The laboratory, complete with its "shining sheath of horizontal glass tubing".

Frank Lloyd Wright was a pioneer of concrete architecture nearly half a century before *Concrete Quarterly* was founded. His Unity Chapel in Oak Park, Illinois, 1908, was one of the first public buildings in America to be built entirely of exposed concrete.[12] As the only material that could be used throughout, for walls, roof, floors and stairs, concrete alone could truly express "unity", Wright explained.[13]

Skip forward 43 years, and Wright, now 83, was still breaking the mould. "In his old age his work has acquired more of the freshness and genuine originality of youth", wrote *Concrete Quarterly* in 1951, "of youth moreover, that still enjoys being something of an 'enfant terrible'. His preoccupation with shapes as shapes, with materials as materials, has led him to some exciting innovations."[14]

The building that had prompted these observations was the Johnson Wax Research Tower, his second building for the company at its campus in Racine, Wisconsin. The shapes were square and circular slabs, cantilevered off a central, cylindrical core; the materials were glass tubes, brick and reinforced concrete. Together, they comprised a radical new approach to tall building.

Wright had long been fascinated by the idea of building a tower with a structure based on organic principles: like a tree, it would have a tap root buried deep in the ground, which would rise into a central trunk-like core with floor plates "branching" off it. The root of the Johnson Wax Research Tower was a reinforced concrete cone extending 50 feet into stiff clay and widening into a 60-foot-diameter ground-floor slab. From this rose the central 14-storey trunk, which housed a large lift, stair and a toilet on each floor. The walls of this concrete core, 7 to 10 inches thick, supported the "branching" floor slabs—alternately a 40-foot-diameter square and a 38-foot-diameter circular mezzanine. Between the floor level and the underside of the next structural slab was a rather claustrophobic 6 feet 5 inches.

One important aspect of this system was that it provided column-free, flexible space—at a time when almost all towers were designed around cellular offices. The spaces were also remarkably uncluttered, thanks to the innovative use of a duct system cast in to the reinforced concrete floor. Because of the resulting complexity of the slabs, casting proved difficult, and the first level took seven weeks to complete. After that, however, "the workmen learned the rhythm and proper timing of the operations and a floor was put up every three weeks".

The structure was wrapped in a skin of Pyrex glass tubes stacked horizontally and supported in an aluminium frame. As with the Unity Temple, Wright was well aware of the symbolic potential of his material choices, seeing the corporate value of a glass tower that would glow at night. "You can raise it like a torch", he told the company president Samuel Curtis Johnson, "to inspire your people around the world."

But for *Concrete Quarterly*, the truly inspiring part of the building lay within. "The structure—trunk, branches, root—has a masterly simplicity, yet this is surely the first time such a natural form has made such a building."

Royal Festival Hall
London, UK
Robert Matthew, Peter Moro,
Leslie Martin

Issue 12, Autumn 1951

Above: The rear, or east, elevation of the Royal Festival Hall, with a temporary facade of asbestos cement sheeting.

Right: The delicate concrete terraces of the Waterloo Bridge Gate and New Schools Pavilion.

Left: Ove Arup's prestressed footbridge on its tapered columns.

Right: The cover of *Concrete Quarterly*'s special issue on the Festival of Britain—the "end of the beginning" of the post-war era.

Below: Typical column elevation of the Arup footbridge, showing position of cables and anchorages.

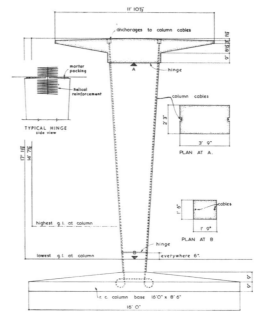

In 1985, the architect Hugh Casson reflected on the turning point of post-war British architecture. "On 27 acres of mud-flat and derelict bomb damage, an army of 27 architects—together with engineers, landscape designers, graphic designers, poets, display artists, sculptors and weavers—mounted a brief city of glass, concrete and aluminium, sparkling, multi-coloured, witty and above all highly successful."[15] The South Bank Exhibition of the Festival of Britain briefly liberated the post-war generation of architects and engineers from the shortages of money, fuel and materials that governed almost all construction, and gave them an amazing opportunity to test out the latest structural and technical advances. "The temporary life of the Exhibition encouraged every sort of experiment", remembered Casson, who was the Festival's Director of Architecture.[16]

It also left some remarkable permanent monuments—not least Robert Matthew, Peter Moro and Leslie Martin's pioneering Royal Festival Hall. "Architecture, since 1851 a dead, or at least a Sleeping Beauty, art, has been moving of late, and we with it", announced *Concrete Quarterly* editor Betty Campbell in autumn 1951. "The buildings of the South Bank confidently appear as the end of the beginning."[17]

It is easy to assume, looking at the early issues of *Concrete Quarterly*, that because concrete was generally grey, so too was the modern world it was being used to shape. The South Bank Exhibition's assault of colour—with sprayed renders of pale blue, primrose, lime green, white and sail red—is therefore immediately striking. This was not, *Concrete Quarterly* hastened to point out, "catchy exhibition stuff", but "genuine building with a sobriety that comes of doing a sound job well".[18] It was still within the spirit of functional architecture, it was just that the function was one that had not been seen for a while: pleasure.

This was the pleasure of visitors (all eight million of them), but also of architects and engineers, "intimately allied... with both enjoying themselves".[19] Gentle rivalry between the various projects would have merely added to the fun. The structures on the site conveyed this enjoyment not only through colour, but through the detail of materials, finishes and through sheer originality. There was the 90-metre-high Skylon, seemingly floating above the ground, the aluminium Dome of Discovery—at the time, the largest dome in the world—and, linking the site together, some highly imaginative use of concrete.

Among the latter were several structures conceived by Ove Arup using one of the era's most exciting developments: prestressing. *Concrete Quarterly* was particularly impressed by the "slim white arrow" of a footbridge that linked Waterloo Bridge with the Festival Hall in three dog-legged spans of 76 feet, 59 feet and 76 feet.

Left: The Committee Room, looking towards Waterloo Bridge Gate Pavilion.

Below: The Festival Hall from the footbridge. The glass facade reveals the internal structure of concrete columns and superimposed foyers and promenades.

Right: A longitudinal section, showing the auditorium raised on its concrete stilts.

Below: Interior of the auditorium.

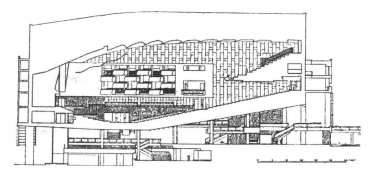

Steel cables running the length of the deck and vertically in the columns provided both strength and delicacy, with anchorages in the top of the deck making the structure into a monolithic whole. The concrete mix of white Portland cement, silver grey Cornish granite and Buckland sand gave an almost sparkling white finish. *Concrete Quarterly* marvelled at its "flyaway, dancing charm".[20]

But the main event lay at the end of the bridge: the Festival Hall itself. Here was a new type of cultural centre—"a home for music, painting, sculpture, theatre, ballet, and good food, in a lovely setting".[21] Such a citadel of the good things in life needed a mighty structure, and here it was: an immense reinforced concrete frame rising from massive piers driven 22 feet into the subsoil—the depth at which the waterlogged site turned to gravel. In a site full of novel construction methods, here was an almost old-fashioned approach to concrete building. The auditorium itself had a double 32-inch-thick wall, made up of two 10-inch leaves of reinforced concrete, cast in situ, with a 1-inch layer of wood wool. The roof likewise was made of two concrete slabs that followed the curve of its steel bowstring trusses. When even the cladding on the riverside facade—of Derbydene fossil stone—added to the fortress-like air, some critics could take no more, deriding the hall as "unnecessarily heavy".

But that, *Concrete Quarterly* felt, was missing the point: the weighty structure was tying the building to the ground in order to let it soar. Viewed from the side elevation, the spaces seemed to float within their frame:

The transparent glass screen shows columns rising from ground to curving roof, carrying foyers, terraces and restaurants and, poised in the centre, isolated and insulated, the precious 'egg' which is the auditorium itself.

Such transparency was democratic, inviting people in, and once there, the effect only intensified: "From the promenades at higher level cantilevered landings seem to float in space, glass on every side, to front, above, below." Even the "egg-like" concert hall seemed to defy gravity—resting as it did on slender 28-foot stilts that transmitted its weight to the mighty foundation piers below. "It seems nowhere linked to the earth—it floats among the lights and the colours, and raised in the centre of this bubble, sound-proofed by space, is the auditorium, centre of it all."

The twin layers of concrete that surrounded the auditorium were perhaps the most important aspect of the structure, sealing in sound and creating a sanctuary from the rapidly modernising world outside. "Inside the auditorium is pure music", wrote *Concrete Quarterly*.

Underground trains may rumble below, steam and electric trains thunder over the bridge alongside, jet planes scream overhead, but all are blotted out while the last frail thread of a violin's high note fades to whisperless silence.

Brynmawr Rubber Factory
Ebbw Vale, UK
Architects Co-operative Partnership,
Ove Arup

Issue 14, Summer 1952

Above: The main production hall—
"a space that is all light and air".

Right: The 'approach' side of the
factory, showing the domes and glass
of the main production hall.

Right: An aerial view of Brynmawr
Rubber Factory.

Below: The interior of the drug room,
roofed with 26 shells of concrete.

Below right: The mill room shells, which
had "an air of almost Victorian daintiness".

Nothing blurred the line between architecture and engineering in the 1950s quite as much as the concrete shell. A form that was given strength through its shape offered exciting possibilities for designers: above all, concrete could suddenly—and rather surprisingly—appear light. "Here, strikingly, is an opportunity, which is being grasped by men of vision, of doing something completely new", wrote *Concrete Quarterly* editor Betty Campbell in 1950.[22]

Nowhere was this opportunity grasped more firmly than at a rubber factory amid the green hills of Ebbw Vale. Brynmawr was intended to be the most modern production facility in the country. No expense was spared as the designers, Architects Co-operative Partnership (ACP) and Ove Arup, set about creating a factory that would set new standards in working conditions and flexibility. "Regularly spaced holes at frequent intervals connect [the ducts] with whatever machine happens to be required", marvelled *Concrete Quarterly*. "The changeover can easily be made during a weekend, without production being held up at all."[23]

But the most remarkable aspect of the building was the structure of its production hall: an uninterrupted main floor of 6,000 square metres beneath nine great domes of white concrete, each resting on four slender V-shaped supports. These domes, 25 metres by 19 metres and just 80 millimetres thick, were "taut as a sheet pinned at the corners and pulling up with the wind". The effect was more spiritual than industrial:

> There have been photographs of this hall. There is one over the page. Maybe you are wiser not to look at it.

> The place it seems, can be captured by no camera's lens. There is suddenly a soaring, a whiteness, a space that is all light and air. A revelation, in fact.

The feat may have been one of engineering, but the effect was down to the seamless union of Arup and ACP's structural and architectural expertise:

> It is possible, of course, to pin it all down to a drawing board and some calculations.... The domes, you may say, have a rise of 8 feet from springing to crown and are only 3 inches thick for all of their span. And you will not forget that 77,000 square feet of floor. You may tell of the fabulous number of square feet of glass that light the area, and your facts will all be there, but there will still be little to tell you how the facts have added up to this floating ship of luminosity in space and sky.

After being used as a production facility by Dunlop until 1982, the building was demolished in 2001. But its magic has endured. Writing in *Concrete Quarterly* in 2016, the Manser Medal-winning architect Chris Loyn recalled stumbling across the empty factory when he was growing up in north Wales.

> I snuck in and wandered beneath its awesome roof. There were nine shells creating a cathedral-like space, which was also very human. It was filled with an ethereal light from the arched clerestory windows—it was phenomenal.[24]

Stockwell Bus Garage
London, UK
Adie, Button and Partners, AE Beer

Issue 20, Winter 1953

Above: A view down the 378-foot length of the garage—"probably the only building of its kind in Europe".

Right: Exterior, showing the double curves of the roof.

Above: An end arch with its cantilevered 'wing' under construction.

Left: The grand sweep of the arches that span the garage's 194-foot width.

By 1953, the red bus had truly taken over the streets of London. The final tram had sidled into history the previous year and now more than 7,000 double-deckers and nearly 900 single-deckers were rumbling through the capital.[25] In south-east London, the trams had been replaced by 200 new buses—which raised the question of where exactly to put them.

The answer was "probably the only building of its kind in Europe"—a vast area, 378 feet long and 194 feet wide, roofed with soaring arches of reinforced concrete and with no internal support of any kind. The architects, Adie, Button and Partners, and consulting engineer AE Beer, had initially considered adopting a shell structure, as used on Brynmawr Rubber Factory, but the need for roof lights that stretched across the width of the building made this unviable.

Instead, an extraordinary sequence of ten mighty arches, 7 feet deep and 26 inches thick, swept across the entire space. Between them were nine doubly curved vaults, at the top of which a series of roof lanterns ran the 140-foot width of the building. The other key elements of the structure were the 'butterfly wings', which cantilevered 22 feet, 6 inches from either end of the arch frames to form 53-foot-high vaults, and a 4-foot-wide H-section beam that wrapped round the entire structure. As *Concrete Quarterly* saw it, the designers had created this immense, column-free space by "simply using to the full those plastic qualities which concrete, alone among building materials, possesses".[26]

Throughout the building, the concrete was left as it was struck from the formwork, with no after treatment apart from rubbing down. The fact that this looked crafted rather than simply unfinished was down to the extreme care that went into both its making and placing. The structure may have been essentially functional, but that didn't mean it couldn't have architectural ambitions. Stockwell Bus Garage's visual impact had been carefully orchestrated; the humble had been made heroic.

1947–1959

Opposite: Interior of the Turin Exhibition Hall.

Below: The Exhibition Hall appeared on the cover of the Spring 1957 issue of *Concrete Quarterly*, which included a special report on northern Italy.

Below right: The first phase of the project had also appeared on the cover of *Concrete Quarterly* in winter 1952.

Right: The roof of the hall under construction. Precast units were mortared together to form corrugations.

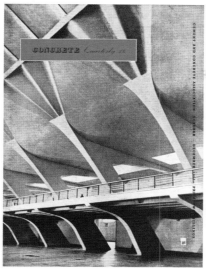

Turin Exhibition Hall
Turin, Italy
Pier Luigi Nervi

Issue 25, Summer 1955

There are some great men whose personality dominates their actual output.... These are the Corbusiers of this world, the Frank Lloyd Wrights. And there are the men whose work speaks for them. Those who say little, write rarely, theorize hardly at all and are content to offer the world a job done. Of these last is Pier Luigi Nervi.[27]

In the 1950s, the pages of *Concrete Quarterly* reverberated with the name Nervi—"a man who combines in one person architect, engineer and contractor, and who sees in this integration the only satisfactory way of constructing". The Cement and Concrete Association (C&CA) even organised three trips to Italy in 1954, 1956 and 1959 for British architects to view his work at first hand. For here was a designer who truly bridged the engineer-architect divide, and did so through one medium: concrete. "In its reactions", *Concrete Quarterly* quoted Nervi as saying, "concrete is a living creature and its ability to adapt itself to difficult, unexpected conditions has always filled me with an astonished admiration". Even his yacht was made from concrete.

As a designer, Nervi embodied the spirit of the age, always searching for "the greatest economy of means and the essential expression of functional truth"—a belief in stripping construction to the bare essentials that he had developed building aircraft hangars for the Italian air force in the 1930s and 1940s. But Nervi also grasped that by delivering structural strength through the use of repeated forms, scaled and curved to meet and resist the forces exerted upon them, he could create buildings of tremendous architectural power.

Nowhere were these values more clearly articulated than on the main exhibition hall at Turin, completed in 1949 and visited by *Concrete Quarterly* six years later. This immense space, 362 feet long and 312 feet in span, was roofed with a mesmerising grid of ferrocement units, each shaped like an inverted U. These were mortared together to form corrugations, and ultimately a single monolithic arch. In-situ reinforced concrete ribs were constructed along the peaks and troughs of the corrugations, and these eventually took over the main structural function. The result was a sight that "never lost its breathtaking impact", *Concrete Quarterly* reported after the third C&CA trip in 1959.[28]

The Turin Exhibition Hall roof was also notable in that it was built without timber formwork—a method that Nervi deplored. He felt that concrete's innate plasticity was shackled by the straight lines imposed by this "ancient form of building" and spent much of his career trying to "liberate" the material from its restrictions.[29] At Turin, the ferrocement units were all precast using moulds themselves made from ferrocement. This was a man, you can't help but feel, who would have used concrete for anything. The only question was, how were the ferrocement moulds moulded?

Warren Tremaine House
Montecito, California, US
Richard Neutra

Issue 26, Autumn 1955

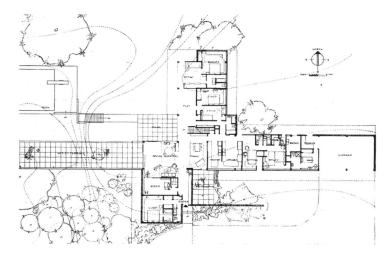

Top: The long terrace, paved with terrazzo.

Above: The dining room terrace at night, with its sandblasted concrete columns.

Left: Ground plan of the bungalow, with the garden "a projection of the interior space".

Right: The view from the entrance,
which shows the structure of the
frames, transverse beams and roof slab.

Below: The open-plan, fully glazed
dining room, with the long terrace
stretching out beyond the wooden
shutters to the left.

California must have seemed an impossibly glamorous place to the average reader of *Concrete Quarterly* in the mid-1950s. Particularly if they had just read issue 26's five-page article "New Industrial Buildings in Hemel Hempstead New Town". Turning the page, they would have encountered a luxurious villa of concrete as white as a Hollywood smile, set in gardens that, even in black and white, looked sickeningly rich with colour. The building in question was the bungalow designed by Richard Neutra for the businessman Warren D Tremaine at Montecito, "where the foothills of the mountains come down to meet the Pacific".[30] We weren't in Hemel any more.

This was one of concrete's first appearances in *Concrete Quarterly* as a material of luxury. In Neutra's hands, it is light, pristine, the roof slab a white sheet "standing out clearly against the dark trees and blue sky" and seemingly floating above the transparent window walls. The roof is lifted above the main beams of the house by a series of transverse beams, with further glazing between, adding to the sense of weightlessness. Beneath this, the main structural concrete frame is warmer in colour and sandblasted—a reference to the exposed boulders that lay throughout the garden.

The use of structural concrete was partly necessitated by the threat of bush fires, but Neutra's treatment of it is subtle. *Concrete Quarterly* noted how a central theme of his houses was "the idea of the garden as a projection of the interior space", but here the roof acts as an understated bridge between the two, its 8-foot cantilever both framing the window walls and shading them from the Californian sun. Moreover, the use of exposed concrete in the interiors—unusual for the time—suggested that the inside space was also a projection of the mountainous landscape. Neutra was struck by how, when used internally, a material such as concrete could be juxtaposed with softer elements such as timber as well as transparent glass—a staple of today's high-end interiors.

It is somehow poignant to imagine the reader of *Concrete Quarterly* in 1955 dwelling momentarily on these photographs of palms, pools, perfectly positioned minimalist furniture and impeccably finished exposed walls before turning to page 23, "Bridges Described to the Pavings Development Group (Concrete and Soil-Cement)"....

Church of La Virgen Milagrosa
Mexico City, Mexico
Félix Candela

Issue 45, Summer 1956

Interior of the Church of La Virgen
Milagrosa—there was a "certain Gothic
sentiment in the treatment", *Concrete
Quarterly* felt.

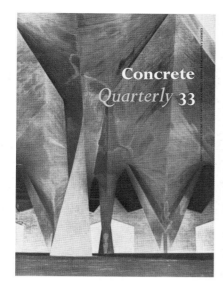

Above: The church appeared on the cover of *Concrete Quarterly* in summer 1957. It would have been the first glimpse many British architects had of Candela's work.

Right: The twisted shapes of the columns and roof cast mysterious shadows across the nave.

Félix Candela was the world's leading exponent of concrete-shell design in the 1950s. Nobody built more of them—3 million square feet in just four years at one point—and nobody did so with such relentless invention.

Concrete was, he reasoned, "akin to the materials of natural shells", and as shells were always double-curved, so too were his structures.[31] In the five years between 1952 and 1957, he built more than 120 buildings in Mexico City alone using the form of the hyperbolic paraboloid—a shape that curves on two axes and has no centre of symmetry. Rarely seen in Europe at this time, the hyperbolic paraboloid could be created by using two formwork systems of straight members lying on a warped parallelogram—thereby avoiding, as Candela noted, "cumbersome and costly arched forms". This was very much the point: Candela's buildings were designed above all for practicality and economy. He cheerfully admitted that most of his clients couldn't have cared less what they looked like.

Yet Candela did care. A trained architect who earned his living as an engineer, he saw no difference between the two disciplines: for him a structure that was both simple and functional was inherently architectural. It followed that his reinforced concrete shells were appropriate not only on the factories and warehouses that were his bread and butter, but also on public buildings and churches.

The Church of La Virgen Milagrosa is a spectacular example. Built in 1955 in the lower-middle-class Colonia Narvarte suburb of Mexico City, it was already world-renowned when *Concrete Quarterly* reviewed it two years later. Candela was entirely responsible for the design, both as architect and engineer. "It was designed in an afternoon, drawn up in a week, and calculated in the process of construction."

The tilted umbrella-shaped shells, formed of four hyperbolic paraboloids, were just 1.5 inches thick and were based on a design Candela had previously used on a wool mill. He had promised the parish a cheap church and ended up losing his own money on it, as he generally did on such 'special jobs'. *Concrete Quarterly* suspected that he "got carried away by the fun of it". The column shapes, Candela said, were dictated by "sentiment" and had to be finished by hand as "the subtle shapes were hardly susceptible of formation by ordinary shuttering and still less by repetition".[32]

The result was a "faintly sinister Gothicism—tinged with that subtly macabre quality one comes to associate with Mexican expression".

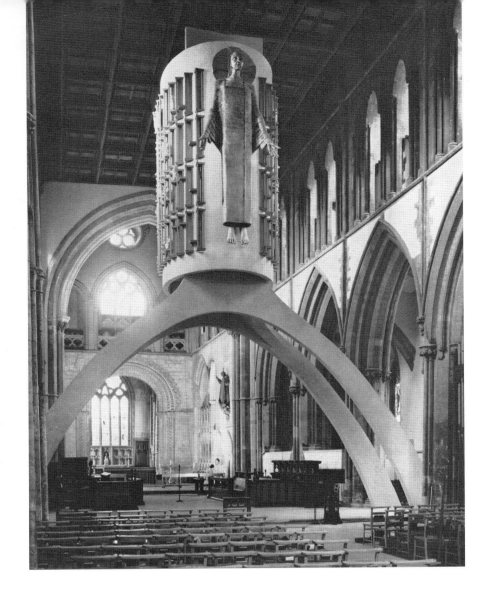

Llandaff Cathedral
Cardiff, UK
George Pace, Ove Arup

Issue 35, Winter 1957

Above: Arup's pulpitum and Epstein's sculpture as seen from the nave.

Right: Looking up at the pulpitum—an interplay of concrete and stone arches.

Below: The initial hand-tooling of
the concrete.

Right: The second stage of tooling,
showing the finer finish obtained with
mechanical equipment.

"Adding to an old building is a ticklish business these days. It has not always been so: the historical conscience is a new thing", wrote *Concrete Quarterly* in 1957.[33] The problem of how to reconstruct historic bomb-damaged buildings provoked fierce debate throughout the 1950s. Basil Spence's Coventry Cathedral had been mired in controversy for years—his design, linking the preserved ruins to a red sandstone-faced building beneath a concrete shell roof, used a mix of traditional and modern construction that seemed to satisfy neither camp.

The architect George Pace faced similar antagonists at Llandaff, which had been badly damaged in a bombing raid on Cardiff in 1941. The main point of contention was the central pulpitum, which, although a revival of a constructional form used in medieval times, was bracingly modern. A parabolic arch of reinforced concrete, 25 feet high, spanned the nave, with a concealed platform for the organ and a sculpture by Jacob Epstein of a distorted Christ in Majesty. The sculpture, with no visible means of support, seemed to have been "released from earth and... floating ever upwards".

But more provocative than the sculpture was the use of concrete. "The arch has been criticized as being 'out of place'", wrote *Concrete Quarterly*, and it knew exactly what that meant: "This looks like another way of saying that concrete, used as concrete and not hiding it, has no place in a stone building." *Concrete Quarterly* countered by pointing out the many layers of construction that made up the true histories of cathedrals:

"Building, rebuilding, alterations and improvements continued throughout the medieval period, every style making its own individual contribution." To criticise Pace's use of modern materials was akin to criticising "the Gothic builders of Llandaff... for not building Norman arches".

The organ arch at Llandaff also shows how quickly concrete was evolving from a functional material to one that could be controlled aesthetically to create precise visual effects. The design team took great care in specifying the finish of the concrete in order to harmonise with the cathedral's limestone structure. An experimental mix was devised containing white Portland cement, khaki "Colorcrete", Derbyshire spar and Portland stone. This was then mechanically tooled to leave a fine finish, free from "misleading ornament".

Far from destroying the cathedral atmosphere, this new layer of history had done much to restore it, *Concrete Quarterly* concluded. "With a design of today and material of today, a sense of aspiration, of movement, is established, in mood as Gothic as the arcades flanking the nave: infinite riches in a little room."

Interior of the auditorium. Rectangular baffles were suspended from the dome to improve the acoustics of the curving form.

Kresge Auditorium
Cambridge, Massachusetts, US
Eero Saarinen

Issue 35, Winter 1957

The three-point thin-shell concrete dome. Concrete buttresses at each corner supported live loads of 1,500 tonnes.

Eero Saarinen was one of the first American architects to fully embrace concrete's ability to create fluid structural forms. His TWA Terminal at Idlewild Airport (now JFK), 1962, captured the sensation of flight in the very framework of the building, with the curving concrete roof flowing seamlessly into its supporting piers. But before that, there was Massachusetts Institute of Technology (MIT)'s Kresge Auditorium—according to *Concrete Quarterly*, "one of the most controversial and striking of contemporary buildings".[34] A concrete dome pinned like a handkerchief at three corners, the concert hall was one of the first examples of concrete thin-shell construction in the US. The roof had a span of 160 feet, a radius of 122 feet and a height above floor level of 50 feet. It was "amazingly light", had no internal columns, and was just 3.5 inches thick at the apex—"thinner in proportion to its area than an egg shell".

As with the TWA Terminal, one senses that Saarinen was more preoccupied with form—and what it evoked—than with function. Functionally speaking, a structural dome seemed a poor choice. As *Concrete Quarterly* observed, "the combination of concave ceiling and curved rear wall tends to focus sound in certain spots and is therefore far from ideal acoustically". But Saarinen believed that "each age must create its own architecture out of its own technology"—and in 1957, concrete shell construction was one of the most exciting technologies

around. Moreover, this was a concert hall at MIT, and a "dome of thin-shell concrete seemed right for a university interested in progressive technology".

The auditorium was a feat of engineering both inside and out. The dome was stiffened with 20-inch-deep edge beams, while the concrete buttresses at each of the three corners had to support live loads of 1,500 tonnes, throwing up problems that required a team of bridge engineers to sort out. Meanwhile, the acoustic difficulties caused by the curving form were solved by an arrangement of rectangular baffles suspended from the dome. "From all accounts the acoustics are now comparable to those of the Royal Festival Hall", wrote *Concrete Quarterly*.

One problem that wasn't solved was the finish of the roof—a thin layer of acrylic plastic mixed with fibreglass and beach sand to give the appearance of weathered limestone. After just a year, this had cracked and was replaced by lead sheeting; in 1979, the current standing-seam copper roofing was put in place. But even if the cladding has changed, the daring of the original vision remains—a vision that, as *Concrete Quarterly* remarked, "cut completely across the conservatism and cobwebs of much contemporary university building".

Hangar One, Gatwick Airport
London, UK
Clive Pascall, Peter Watson,
Alan Harris

Issue 37, Summer 1958

Above: The prestressed, post-tensioned, triangular space frame spanned the 104-foot width of the Transair hangar.

Right: The Summer 1958 issue featured a special report on the opening of Gatwick, London's second airport.

Concrete *Quarterly* 37

"The second half of the 20th century is to be the era of prestressed concrete", declared editor Betty Campbell in 1950. "Here is a new call to men of imagination and vision: let architects of an enquiring mind... explore its possibilities."[35]

In the 1950s, the potential of prestressed concrete appeared almost limitless. The technique, developed by the French engineer Eugène Freyssinet in the late 1920s, worked by stretching high-tensile steel wires through the concrete and releasing them when it had hardened, exerting an upward force and placing the concrete under permanent compression. It was first used in Britain during the Second World War, largely as a replacement for timber in railway sleepers, but engineers soon realised that its high strength and ability to span considerable distances, using comparatively little material, could revolutionise various types of construction.

For *Concrete Quarterly*, prestressed concrete was "that strange resilient material that has all the qualities concrete never dreamed of".[36] Early issues of the magazine included prestressed bridges in France, the Netherlands and Belgium, a prestressed Swedish paper mill and a prestressed cotton factory in Devon. And when London's second airport, Gatwick, opened in the summer of 1958, the building that the magazine chose to focus on was not the main terminal—even though it made an "arresting impression" with its acres of exposed concrete—but a hangar with an improbably lace-like prestressed roof.

Hangar One belonged to Transair, the first airline to land at Gatwick and the first to base its fleet, comprising 12 Dakmaster and three Viscounts, there. Designed by architects Clive Pascall and Peter Watson with engineer Alan Harris, the hangar had to be large enough to service two or three aircraft at a time. With steel still scarce in post-war Britain, the answer lay with a precast concrete post-tensioned triangular space frame, which spanned the width of the 38,000-square-foot building. The lattice of incredibly slender ribs and nodes was "an inspiring example of the strength and elegance which can be achieved by a combination of precasting and prestressing", wrote *Concrete Quarterly*. The relatively small structural loads allowed the entire frontage to be filled with two power-operated folding sliding doors, providing two clear spans for aircraft of 140 feet. A continuous beam over the doors was supported by three prestressed concrete columns.

As well as being strong and elegant, the frames proved cost-effective—solid concrete beams would have meant increased weight and therefore additional expense. Prestressed concrete, combining innovation with efficiency, seemed to be the perfect material for the brave new world of commercial aviation. "The entire project at Gatwick reflects the attitudes of the aircraft world", wrote *Concrete Quarterly*. "To look forward, and to combine enthusiasm with economy." Of course, enthusiasm and economy aren't always the friend of architecture: as the imperatives of airlines have changed, Gatwick has remained in an almost constant state of redevelopment. Hangar One hung on until 2013, when it was quietly and unceremoniously demolished.

Roehampton Lane Estate
London, UK
London County Council

Issue 39, Winter 1958

Above: Pilotis with a board-marked finish
frame a view of the adjacent slab block.

Right: An aerial view of the estate looking
east towards Roehampton village.

Far left: A 12-storey point block in the course of construction.

Left: The separate flats were clearly legible from the outside.

"Here is a totally opposite concept of a town: the open space—the tower in a park."[37] *Concrete Quarterly*, like many in the architectural and planning professions, spent much of the 1950s considering the question of density, and whether the compact street-and-square layout of terraced housing was fit for purpose in the rapidly expanding cities of post-war Britain. For *Concrete Quarterly*, part of the answer lay with tower blocks set in landscaped parkland, or 'open planning'. The high-rise life offered improved air quality, tranquillity and views, freeing up space for trees and lawns. In 1958, the word 'estate' carried no negative connotations with the public—indeed, *Concrete Quarterly* thought it might be "soothing" to present these vast developments as something separate from the wider town. But *Concrete Quarterly* also foresaw the problems with this form of development to be used without variation. "Open planning alone can be as monotonous as anything else, and leave more people dissatisfied", it wrote. "Mixed development gives it life." In other words, even in 1958, people could see the need for shops, pubs, community facilities and other types of housing to make tower living work.

Nowhere was this approach better exemplified than at Roehampton Lane, the largest of the post-war housing estates designed and developed by the London County Council (LCC):

> Whether one views the Roehampton scheme from the top floor balcony of one of the point blocks, with its breathtaking view into the heart of Surrey, or from a bench in Richmond Park, one realizes that this is something more than a purely architectural concept: it is a design for living.

The LCC Architects' Department was arguably the most prolific practice in the country in the 1950s, first under the leadership of Robert Matthew and then Leslie Martin. By 1953, it had 1,773 staff, and the figures that passed through it read like a *Who's Who* of British post-war architecture, including Peter Moro, Colin St John Wilson, Percy Johnson-Marshall and Alison and Peter Smithson.[38] At Roehampton Lane, a team including Colin Lucas and John Partridge designed a diverse scheme comprising fifteen 12-storey point blocks; five 11-storey maisonette slab blocks; a lower development of four-storey maisonettes over shops; two- and three-storey terrace houses and single-storey houses for older people; as well as 26 shops, two doctors' surgeries, a pub, two churches, a nursery, primary and secondary school, a community centre for old people and—a particularly utopian touch—roadside allotments.

The LCC had purchased 305 acres in Roehampton in 1948 and had already developed three estates there: Ashburton, Ackroydon and Alton East. But the site at Roehampton Lane was the most promising of all. There were oaks, elms, cedars—"indeed, almost every imaginable type of English tree"—several historic houses, and views over Richmond Park, Roehampton village and, to the north, a bank of trees above a meadow. There were also plenty of variations in levels for the architects to work with—the terrace houses were arranged on some of the steeper slopes "with all the charm of a Mediterranean hillside village".

For *Concrete Quarterly* the star attractions were the two groups of 100-foot-high point blocks, the landmarks to which everything else related. Point blocks were slender towers with three or four flats on each floor that were first used in pre-war central Europe. Often raised on pilotis, they were practical where foundations were difficult and offered plenty of natural light. They were less common in Britain, but tended to be used where land was expensive or where there was a desire to retain mature trees.[39] One significant difference with other types of block housing was that they were directly related to the human scale, with the separate flats clearly legible from the outside.

The point blocks at Roehampton weren't quite like any that the LCC had built before—a consequence of the Architects' Department working in discrete teams, even on neighbouring sites such as these ones. While the in-situ concrete frames of the Alton East blocks had been faced with light grey bricks, at Roehampton Lane there was concrete inside and out, with an exposed external finish of Dorset shingle and Derbyshire spar. The Roehampton Lane architects were young, idealistic and had recently visited Le Corbusier's latest work, the Unité d'Habitation in Marseille. It showed.

The facades were built using precast concrete cladding panels, either one-storey high or two bays across for balconies. These marked "the extremity of each living unit", bringing the required human scale to the blocks, but were uncompromisingly monolithic. The panels were reprised on the even more overtly Corbusian slab blocks and the maisonettes, bringing a sense of unity, if not subtlety, to the scheme. *Concrete Quarterly* found little intimidating in the finish, noting "a warm buff-grey effect close to, although from a distance the overall effect is silver-grey and a good deal lighter in tone than... the Alton Estate".

Such concrete estates would not always be viewed so benignly. Within seven years, Roehampton Lane had become the backdrop for the film adaptation of Ray Bradbury's bleakly futuristic *Fahrenheit 451*. But its original buildings are now scheduled for regeneration and a master plan proposes to add even more housing to the site. Like some other early estates, it has journeyed from utopian to dystopian to semi-gentrification. The test will be whether it can once again offer the design for future living that *Concrete Quarterly* saw in 1958.

UNESCO Headquarters
Paris, France
Marcel Breuer, Pier Luigi Nervi, Bernard Zehrfuss

Issue 40, Spring 1959

Above: An end wall of the Congress Hall building with the 'Salle des pas perdus' linking it to the Secretariat.

Right: A committee room, with one of the vast external concrete walls forming a backdrop.

The concrete wall formed a monumental curtain behind the Congress Hall's rostrum.

Le Corbusier should have built the headquarters for UNESCO. At least that's what a number of leading architects believed, including José Luís Sert, Walter Gropius and, needless to say, Le Corbusier. Instead the commission went to a suitably international team of Hungarian-American Marcel Breuer, Italian Pier Luigi Nervi and Frenchman Bernard Zehrfuss. Le Corbusier found the resulting design banal, but for *Concrete Quarterly* it was "genuine magic".[40]

There was a reason why Le Corbusier was so disgruntled: this was one of the most prestigious architectural projects in post-war Europe, in one of its grandest locations, opposite the École Militaire on Place de Fontenoy. Whatever was built, it would immediately become a defining image of the new Europe.

The complex that Breuer, Nervi and Zehrfuss created was emphatically new. The main Secretariat building was a seven-storey concrete-framed block in a curving Y-shape, resting on 76 splayed pilotis. While the Place de Fontenoy facade was politely clad in travertine panels, the other sides were wrapped in concrete brise-soleil fins and balcony-like louvres between each floor. The hand of Nervi was clearly detectable in two entrance canopies—one a thin trapezoidal slab supported by three slim, tapered columns that showed "politeness to neighbours and distinct personality at the same time"; the other a double-curved structure that flared up in a 33-foot cantilever, with which *Concrete Quarterly* was less taken. "It is unfortunate that this structure, which looks as though it should have been as light and airy as a sheet of paper, should in fact be so ponderous."

For *Concrete Quarterly*, the real magic lay in the complex's second building, the Congress Hall. "The first sight of the Congress Hall is like a blast of trumpets—a shock of delight and wonder." This was partly due to its virtuosic structure, with roof and raking end walls made up of 12 inverted V-sections, creating shapes like the folds of an accordion both internally and externally. The deep Vs of the walls gently flattened towards the ground like a vast geolithic curtain, while in the longer spans of the roof they gave way to curving concrete shells that could better cope with the compressive stresses.

But more impressive than the structure was the quality of the concrete finish itself—perhaps one of the first instances where architects strove to highlight the craftsmanship inherent in the formed material. Clauses were inserted in the brief specifically relating to the concrete. It was stated from the outset that "the reinforced concrete structure has not only a constructional function but also a very important architectural one", and that "plywood or metal forms must not be used; the pattern of the boards and their small irregularities of surface form an architectural element which must be retained". Nervi overcame his dislike of timber formwork. The contractor, Fourre and Rhodes-Dumez, adopted a rigorous approach, confining itself "to a strict adherence to the rules governing the art of our profession". Formwork was made rigid and watertight, reinforcement was fixed carefully, and the concrete used always conformed to that specified.

The result was a showcase of different concrete techniques. "There is some splendid bush-hammering with smooth clean arrises; there is concrete straight from the timber forms; there is concrete... lightly rubbed down." The effect was most striking from the foyer's central row of columns, which swelled from a narrow rectangle at the top to a rounded section at the base shaped like a boat's hull (in fact, they were cast in narrow-boarded timber formwork made by naval carpenters). It was like standing "within a piece of abstract sculpture, formed by an interplay of planes and textures, expressed in concrete of a dazzling quality". One footbridge partially obscured a mural by Picasso—but for *Concrete Quarterly*, that didn't lessen the artistic effect.

Right: Detail of a piloti, showing the change in section through the height.

Below: Evening sunlight falling across the piazza, lighting the concrete of the pilotis.

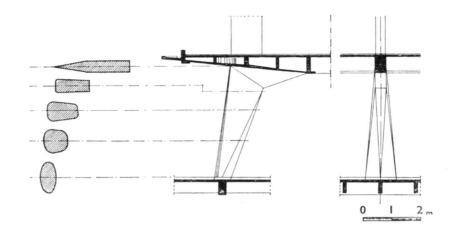

THE WORLD RECAST: 70 BUILDINGS FROM 70 YEARS OF *CONCRETE QUARTERLY*

Above: Different concrete finishes in the Congress Hall: lightly rubbed down on the left, bush-hammered on the right.

Left: The view from the Congress Hall, over 'Salle des pas perdus' to the Secretariat.

1947–1959

1   Casson, Hugh, "Britain Gets Going Again", *Concrete Quarterly*, Issue 144, 1985, p 16.

2   Campbell, Betty, "Editorial", *Concrete Quarterly*, Issue 12, Autumn 1951, p 1.

3   "Houses Made Here!", *Concrete Quarterly*, Issue 3, Summer 1948, p 20.

4   "The Factories at Crawley New Town", *Concrete Quarterly*, Issue 14, Summer 1952, p 2.

5   "Nervi", *Concrete Quarterly*, Issue 25, Summer 1955, p 28.

6   "The Rubber Factory at Brynmawr", *Concrete Quarterly*, Issue 14, Summer 1952, p 29.

7   "Nervi", p 20.

8   Campbell, Betty, "Editorial", *Concrete Quarterly*, Issue 7, Winter 1949, p 1.

9   Campbell, "Editorial", Issue 7, p 1.

10   "If All Mines Were Like This: The Triumph of Comrie Pit", *Concrete Quarterly*, Issue 2, Spring 1948, p 3.

11   Manzoni, Sir Herbert J, "Birmingham Inner Ring Road", *Concrete Quarterly*, Issue 49, Summer 1961, p 2.

12   Lipman, Jonathan, *Frank Lloyd Wright and the Johnson Wax Buildings*, New York: Rizzoli, 1986.

13   McCarter, Robert, "Unity Temple", *Architecture 3: Frank Lloyd Wright*, London: Phaidon, 1999.

14   "Frank Lloyd Wright: A versatile architect and his latest work", *Concrete Quarterly*, Issue 10, Spring 1951, pp 7–11. All subsequent quotations in this section are from the same article.

15   Casson, "Britain Gets Going Again", p 19.

16   Casson, "Britain Gets Going Again", p 20.

17   Campbell, "Editorial", Issue 12, Autumn 1951, p 1.

18   Campbell, "Editorial", Issue 12, p 1.

19   Campbell, "Editorial", Issue 12, p 2.

20   "The Prestressed Concrete Footbridge on the South Bank", *Concrete Quarterly*, Issue 12, Autumn 1951, p 12.

21   "The Royal Festival Hall, South Bank", *Concrete Quarterly*, Issue 12, Autumn 1951, pp 16–21. All subsequent quotations in this section are from the same article.

22   Campbell, Betty, "Editorial", *Concrete Quarterly*, Issue 8, 1950, p 1.

23   "The Rubber Factory at Brynmawr", *Concrete Quarterly,* Issue 14, Summer 1952, pp 26–31. All subsequent quotations in this section are from the same article.

24   Loyn, Chris, "Lasting Impression", *Concrete Quarterly*, Issue 258, 2016, p 19.

25   Christopher, John, *The London Bus Story*, Stroud: The History Press, 2009.

26   "Stockwell Bus Garage", *Concrete Quarterly*, Issue 20, Winter 1953, pp 10–14.

27   "Pier Luigi Nervi", *Concrete Quarterly*, Issue 25, Summer 1955, pp 20–28.

28   "Italian Visit 1959", *Concrete Quarterly*, Issue 42, Autumn 1959, p 50.

29   "Pier Luigi Nervi", pp 20–28.

30   "New Industrial Buildings in Hemel Hempstead New Town", *Concrete Quarterly*, Issue 26, Autumn 1955, pp 14–17. All subsequent quotations in this section are from the same article.

31   "Felix Candela", *Concrete Quarterly*, Issue 33, Summer 1957, pp 19–28. All subsequent quotations in this section are from the same article, with the exception of footnote 32.

32   "Felix Candela", *Concrete Quarterly*, Issue 42, Summer 1959, p 5.

33   "Llandaff Cathedral Organ Arch", *Concrete Quarterly*, Issue 35, Winter 1957. All subsequent quotations in this section are from the same article.

34   "Massachusetts Institute of Technology", *Concrete Quarterly*, Issue 35, Winter 1957. All subsequent quotations in this section are from the same article.

35   Campbell, Betty, "Editorial", *Concrete Quarterly*, Issue 8, 1950, p 1.

36   "The new airport at Gatwick", *Concrete Quarterly*, Issue 37, Summer 1958, pp 2–10. All subsequent quotations in this section are from the same article.

37   "Roehampton Lane housing estate", *Concrete Quarterly*, Issue 39, Winter 1958. All subsequent quotations in this section are from the same article.

38   Harwood, Elain, *Space, Hope and Brutalism*, London: Yale University Press, 2016, p 67.

39   Harwood, *Space, Hope and Brutalism*, p 22.

40   "UNESCO Headquarters, Paris", *Concrete Quarterly*, Issue 40, Spring 1959, pp 27–36. All subsequent quotations in this section are from the same article.

Government Building
Oslo, Norway
Erling Viksjø, Carl Nesjar
Issue 44, Spring 1960

In 1961, the International Union of Architects came to Britain. It was the first time that the body had held its Congress in the country, and for *Concrete Quarterly* the inference was clear: British architecture was suddenly of global interest. We now had "a wealth of good buildings that we in our country are able to show to our visitors from abroad", wrote editor Betty Campbell.[1]

British architecture had a spring in its step, and this new-found confidence was about to be released on an era that the historian Barnabas Calder has described as "objectively, almost measurably, the most exciting and artistically rich period in which to be an architect".[2] This was the heroic age of concrete architecture. The demands of the post-war years were suddenly being met by a torrent of cheap energy and a building boom, with the dominant style being bold, primitively sculptural, robust—in short, 'brutalist'.

The sense of robustness was part of the point—a reaction both to the destruction of the war and to the perceived ephemerality of the modern. New architecture in lighter materials had, Campbell wrote,

like the modern American automobile, a built-in obsolescence, designed to disappear after a few years' use, and

leading to an entirely new and rootless way of life. Maybe it is the life of the future. We rather hope not.[3]

But 1960s concrete was not all about brute force. At Nottingham Playhouse, Peter Moro was demonstrating how the material—cast in situ and impeccably board-marked—could form the basis of a new language in civic architecture. Used alongside materials such as timber, glass and soft carpet, it could be both imposing and classless—an aesthetic for the times. Meanwhile, at Hugh Casson's London Zoo Elephant House, the pachydermal curves and ribs showed that 1960s modernism could even be witty.

Not that concrete had all the answers. The flip side of the building boom was a housing shortage that was reaching crisis proportions. Although, in 1962, some 300,000 houses were being built each year, this was 100,000 short of the country's immediate needs.[4] The best way to solve this was unclear, and *Concrete Quarterly*, rather than simply championing the cause of fast, cheap concrete solutions, was as anxious as many others that we might be rushing headlong down the wrong path. By 1966, editor George Perkin was wondering whether the modernist utopia of high-rise living was in danger of toppling:

> More often than not these spaces have proved bleak, windy and unlovable.... Have we faced the fact that high buildings do not always create space around them? Corbusier had thought they would, but in fact we now find that much of this space has to be devoted to car parks.[5]

It was a reminder that architects' confidence could be misplaced. But that same confidence was also responsible for some of the twentieth century's most exhilarating buildings.

Government Building
Oslo, Norway
Erling Viksjø, Carl Nesjar

Issue 44, Spring 1960

Above: The 15-storey concrete-framed tower of the H-block.

Right: Detail of a gable end wall. The repeating pattern was sandblasted through rubber stencils.

Left: Bold figures designed by Kai Fjell decorate a wall in the building's entrance foyer.

Below: A staircase wall, treated with an abstract design and cast with black cement.

Liquid when cast, stone-like when set, concrete always offered exciting possibilities as a sculptural material—a common ground on which artist and architect could meet. Throughout the 1960s, British artists such as William Mitchell and Eric Peskett were creating murals for buildings as diverse as London's Northern Polytechnic and Liverpool Roman Catholic Cathedral. Meanwhile, in Norway, the concrete canvas had drawn the biggest name in twentieth-century art: Pablo Picasso.

Picasso had been attracted by Naturbetong (natural concrete), a variation on the material that had been developed by the Norwegian modernist architect Erling Viksjø. The casting process involved filling the formwork with large pieces of rounded aggregate—often river gravel—before piping in a mortar of cement, water, fine sand and various admixtures. The mortar would form a smooth surface to the concrete, and crucially would still be fairly soft when the forms were removed.

It was at this point that the artist stepped in. Viksjø had worked with the painter and sculptor Carl Nesjar since the mid-1950s on a surface treatment for Naturbetong that involved sandblasting the outer layer of mortar to leave decorative line patterns in the exposed aggregate. The technique was more sgraffito than sculpture but, wrote Concrete Quarterly, "in the hands of the right person, [it] has as many possibilities as the pencil or graver in the hands of the artist".

Viksjø had won the commission for the new Government Building in Oslo back in 1939, but the project had been delayed by the war and it wasn't until 1957 that the structure was complete. Naturbetong had been used throughout the 15-storey tower, known as the H-block, and Nesjar now assembled some of the best young Norwegian painters to decorate the gable ends, interior walls and stairwells. But his real coup was in luring Picasso: the painter was so excited by the possibilities of sandblasting that he offered three sketches free of charge, as well as creating a totem-like concrete sculpture for Viksjø's back garden.

Whereas the Norwegian artists who worked on the Government Building favoured abstract, geometric patterns, Picasso's works were more naturalistic, and included a somewhat out-of-place beach volleyball scene. Nesjar projected the master's drawings onto a wall using a lantern before sandblasting the lines into the concrete.

In 1969, Viksjø added a second building to the complex, a low-rise Y-shaped block reminiscent of the UNESCO Headquarters in Paris. Again, Picasso provided designs for the sandblasted walls: the three-storey The Fishermen mural on the facade and, in the lobby, a seagull, eyes bulging, swooped to snatch a fish from the ocean. Concrete Quarterly had long supported "the strong movement afoot to bring the artist—and consequently more richness—into the design of twentieth century buildings".[6] Picasso, it seemed, was leading the charge.

There's a sad irony to the story of post-war concrete artwork. As decorative art was elevated in status and became an integral part of architecture, it actually became less permanent, its fate entwined with that of the building. Many of Mitchell's best works, including Northern Polytechnic, are no longer with us. Meanwhile, the future of The Fishermen, perhaps Picasso's finest Naturbetong mural, hangs in the balance after the building was seriously damaged in the 2011 Norway terrorist attacks. Despite public protests and pleas from heritage groups, the Y-block faces demolition to make way for a new government complex.

Presidential Palace
Brasília, Brazil
Oscar Niemeyer

Issue 45, Summer 1960

Above: The approach to the President's Palace, with its 'swan' columns clad in white marble.

Right: The Palace under construction.

Below: The President's chapel closes the vista along the Palace terrace.

Right: The terrace mirroring the slender columns after a sudden downpour.

In *Concrete Quarterly*'s early years, nowhere on Earth held such fascination as Brazil. The magazine wrote in 1953:

> It is the freedom and sensitiveness of Brazilian architecture, allied as it is to a clean purity of line and sound structural principles, which is Brazil's great contribution to contemporary architecture.... It is something which, without being a copy-book, should be an inspiration. [7]

Concrete Quarterly made it its mission to spread that inspiration to its British readership: in its very first issue, amid the reports on rural housing and advances in sewage disposal, are four pages on Rio de Janeiro's "bold and ingenious" architecture, including Lúcio Costa and Oscar Niemeyer's tropical office block for the Ministry of Education and Health.

Brazil's architects had been in thrall to Corbusian modernism in the 1930s and, unlike their European counterparts, their progress was relatively unhindered by the war. "These men were creating a new architecture while we, intent on other matters, knew nothing of the miracle that was taking place."[8] By the 1950s, this "miracle" was most obviously revealed by a playful mastery of reinforced concrete quite unlike any other architecture anywhere else in the world.

> The Brazilian architect is... gloriously freed from the mystique of pure functionalism that was tending to paralyse the development of individual art. Notice, for example, the sculptural—the plastic—quality of so much Brazilian architecture. Notice its love of the curve, of colour.[9]

The name of Niemeyer in particular began to crop up more and more regularly: his Church of St Francis of Assisi and Club Libanais in Pampulha; his Copan tower in São Paulo; his Boavista Bank headquarters in Rio.

But it wasn't until 1960 that *Concrete Quarterly* got the chance to visit Brazil. Fortunately this coincided with the most ambitious project of Niemeyer's career—indeed, one of the most ambitious architectural projects of all time. In 1955, the new president Juscelino Kubitschek had decided to build an entirely new capital city from scratch. Brasília was "the product of two brains only: the plan, Lucio Costa's, the buildings, Oscar Niemeyer's".[10] In just five years, it had become a reality—albeit with plenty of work still to do: the city was, *Concrete Quarterly* noted on arrival,

> a place of widely scattered buildings, red earth with runnels of water shining in the sun, red mud sparkling, and, arched over all, the immense blue dome of the sky piled with great white mountains of cloud.

Already risen from the red earth, however, were some of Niemeyer's great showpieces. There was the pure abstract sculpture of the government buildings: the twin towers of the Secretariat, the balancing bowl of the Chamber of Deputies, the dome of the Senate. And then there was the Presidential Palace. It is striking how the language with which *Concrete Quarterly* described this building was totally different to that used for any of the other great buildings of the 1960s. The facade was "serene"; the columns "swans", their slender neck-like stems rising from a smooth mirrored pool and "festooned along the veranda". The sinuous concrete curves of the terrace were "wonderfully unthickened" by their white marble cladding.

With projects such as the Presidential Palace, Niemeyer had brought entirely new forms to concrete architecture. The material had not so much turned a corner as decided that corners were optional.

1960–1969

Pirelli Tower
Milan, Italy
Gio Ponti, Pier Luigi Nervi

Issue 51, Winter 1961

The tower's slim, tapering profile relied
on two triangular cores at each end of
the building and four concrete piers
rising through the middle.

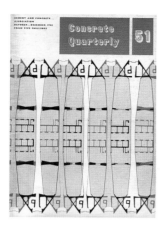

The Winter 1961 cover showed a graphic by Ponti based on the tower's plan.

Left: The top floor of the building, with its split piers and beams in exposed concrete.

Above: Looking down from the top of the building—at the time the tallest concrete structure in Europe.

Concrete Quarterly visited Italy several times in the late 1950s, a time when the post-war Italian economic miracle was in full swing and it almost looked as though the country could teach America a thing or two about building skyscrapers.

> The upward is everywhere: new housing estates are all blocks of flats, generally four to eight storeys high, and blocks of offices are slim elegant towers giving the cities a skyline as varied and interesting as the spires of the City churches gave to London in the eighteenth century.[11]

Of these, the 32-storey Pirelli Tower was indisputably the slimmest and most elegant.

The key to the tower's refinement was its plan: narrow, tapering at both ends, giving it the sleekness of an upturned airplane wing. This had been laid down by the architect, Gio Ponti, but the job of making it stand up went (as with so many innovative European structures) to Pier Luigi Nervi. Nervi designed a slender reinforced concrete frame—at the time, the tallest in Europe—in which the entire 60,000-tonne weight of the building was conveyed to the ground through four massive concrete piers, placed at approximately third points in the length of the building, and two triangular cores at both of the tapered ends. The four triangular boxes were also designed to take service lifts and all ducting the full height of the building, thereby enabling another of Ponti's requirements: as much free, uninterrupted space as possible.

This posed more challenges for Nervi and his team. Large-span concrete floors concentrated loads on the eight structural elements, ensuring that there was no need for intermediate supports of any kind. However, the largest of these spans was some 79 feet, and with a floor depth of 29.5 inches—a ratio of 1:35—this raised fears of significant deflection. Provision was made for prestressing the longitudinal beams after erection, but in the event Nervi's structural analysis proved spot on. The maximum deflection was just a quarter of an inch.

Inside, all was as light and cool as the graceful, glazed exterior suggested. But Ponti chose to reveal the tower's mighty frame both in the bush-hammered auditorium on the lobby floors and on the top three floors, "a magnificent open space" where the rough concrete piers met the final level of beams, and the roof seemingly floated above. "Open to the wind, and with fabulous views over the city", wrote *Concrete Quarterly*, "here one is fully conscious of the strength of bone and sinew that has gone into this elegant structure".[12]

Monastery of La Tourette
Éveux, France
Le Corbusier

Issue 53, Summer 1962

Above: Pools of light from the concrete
funnels above illuminate the altars
of the side chapel while priests
celebrate mass.

Right: Roof structures, in a
rough grass walk, form abstract
concrete sculptures.

Below: The monastery from the south west. The two rows of cell balconies at the top are set over communal rooms below.

Right: Detail of the south-west corner showing the robust treatment of rough rendered and board-marked in-situ concrete.

Le Corbusier was the undisputed master of raw concrete, or *béton brut*, and the Monastery of La Tourette near Lyon was concrete at its rawest. For a place of religious observance, it was weirdly, shockingly militaristic. As the historian Adrian Forty put it: "It is hard not to look at the outer wall of the church and the bastions and not think of a blockhouse."[13]

It is not every day that one comes face-to-face with an acknowledged beast of Brutalism, and *Concrete Quarterly's* George Perkin approached the monastery with anxious excitement when he visited in the summer of 1962. He wrote:

It looms up suddenly with powerful impact against a background of trees.... At this point, the first of many shocks is administered: the visitor sees nothing more exciting than the blank north wall of the church in uncompromisingly rough board-marked concrete.... Can the master be having us all on?[14]

Around the corner, another shock:

A facade of strange rhythms with a double row of stark rectangular openings at the top, set over three storeys of irregularly spaced vertical fins, and several bizarre protuberances. It is certainly quite unlike anything one has ever seen before.

Then, further surprises as he came to the other two elevations:

Openings at the top, fins below, protuberances everywhere— except that the lower floor is replaced by stilts to take up the sharply rising ground. This, at least, is a familiar Corbusier trait.

Inside too, Perkin found little sanctuary. Here was

an uncompromising austerity and simplicity, taken to astonishing limits. Board-marked concrete is left unadorned throughout, and it is concrete of a roughness to which we are not accustomed in this country.... All the imperfections of workmanship are laid bare (a reflection of human nature?); nothing is concealed anywhere. Even the service pipes are exposed in the corridors and painted in blues and ochres.

Gradually, however, Perkin began to see something more to the building than unfamiliar shapes and rough surfaces, "something as potent and evocative as a waft of incense from a church door". The strange protuberances he had seen rising from the chapel roof were actually light funnels, filtering "astonishing pools of yellow, red and blue" obliquely into the side chapels. The slender vertical fins of precast concrete in the long windows of the communal rooms gave "an effect of rippling water, with their irregular spacings". Even the rare walls of smoothed concrete opposite where each monk sat in his cell took on a strange, intangible significance: "Could it be a moment of rest, akin to what Corbusier calls an 'interval of silence'?"

Shock had given way to a kind of awe.

One begins to see that this monastery—contrary to what one had at first supposed—has a great deal to do with early medieval patterns and traditions. Is there not perhaps a similarity in feeling, a basic dignity, an austere beauty— in short, a true reflection of monastic life throughout the ages? And is this not, above all, a building designed for human beings?

Opposite: The students' oratory in the courtyard—a projecting cube of concrete topped by a steep pyramid.

Left: The monks at prayer in the church, facing each other in two rows. Walls of rough board-marked concrete tower above them to exclude the outside world.

University of Sussex
Sussex, UK
Basil Spence, Ove Arup

Issue 53, Summer 1962

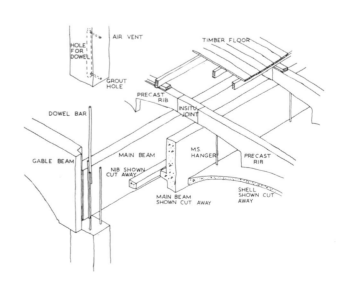

Above: The "pure concrete skeleton" of College House, photographed in the winter of 1961.

Right: Diagram showing the structural system used throughout the university buildings.

Right: The regular unbroken rhythm of vaults in the Physics Building, each spanning 20 feet.

Below: A single vault spans the 40-foot-wide refectory, constructed from precast beams covered with Siporex slabs.

By 1962, higher education was feeling the aftershocks of the post-war baby boom. In a *Concrete Quarterly* article titled "Exploding Universities Build in Concrete", writer Nicolette Franck expressed the urgency of the situation:

At present this country provides fewer university places in proportion to the population than any country in Western Europe. To maintain even this level, student numbers would have to double by the following year.[15]

New universities had been set up in Norwich, York and Sussex, and there were more to follow in Canterbury, Colchester, Coventry and Lancaster. The sheer volume of expansion was, Franck noted, bringing about "a breakthrough in the 'traditionalist' attitude to architecture of university authorities, and there is already interesting work to be seen that speaks of its own time".[16]

Nowhere spoke more eloquently of its time than Basil Spence's campus for the University of Sussex outside Brighton. Arranged as a close-knit horizontal development of quadrangles, it was already "something of a landmark in modern architecture" when *Concrete Quarterly* inspected progress on the first two buildings—College House and the Physics Department—in the summer of 1962. Of particular interest was its unusual precast concrete structure, devised by Ove Arup, which brought unprecedented levels of speed, efficiency and economy to Spence's design.

The design was distilled into a few repeating precast elements: three sizes of columns, for example, and three spans of barrel vaults (the campus' recurring theme). Facades were made of precast panels, strongly board-marked by Canadian Douglas fir, and infills of rich red brick. Knapped flints were embedded in some of the walls, echoing the "fine old tradition of Sussex flint walling". A casting yard was set up on site, which meant that finished elements merely had to be craned into position. Only the foundations and retaining walls were cast in situ.

The vault units were particularly ingenious. Arup came up with a way of casting them integrally with their transverse beams, forming a unit that looked like a huge, bowed table turned upside-down. The beams were made first, then placed over curved steel forms onto which the 2.5-inch-thick vaults were cast, with the reinforcement of the two elements hooked together. After the units had been moved into position, all services were discreetly channelled between the vault and the timber floors above.

For *Concrete Quarterly*, there was "distinct poetry in this concrete skeleton". Not that skeleton was quite the right word—the vaults were actually suspended ceilings, and not part of the structure at all. This, *Concrete Quarterly* conceded, might prove "a bone of contention" for the purists, particularly as they were expressed on the facades in the manner of a structural element. "To some this will seem an extravagant kind of architecture but then, as Mr Ove Arup pointed out during a site visit, the extravagant look is essential to good architecture."

1960–1969

A completed vault unit being craned into position.

THE WORLD RECAST: 70 BUILDINGS FROM 70 YEARS OF *CONCRETE QUARTERLY*

The interior of the Physics Building, showing the smooth concrete soffits of the vaults from the steel forms.

Above: The site casting yard, showing precast rib beams being placed over curved steel forms prior to casting the vaults.

Left: Precast facing units, with subtle board markings, close the vaults to College House.

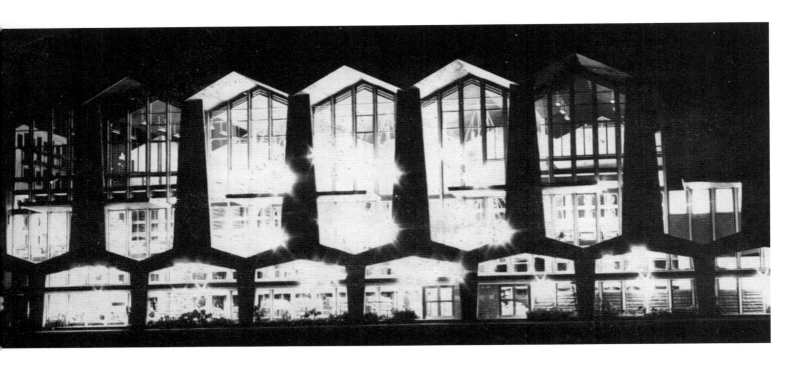

Great Library, University of Nairobi
Nairobi, Kenya
Anthony M Chitty, Ove Arup

Issue 60, Spring 1964

Above: Lights shining out of the library's glazed facade at night.

Right: And the same facade by day, showing the folded plate roof and the horizontal and vertical brise-soleil.

Opposite left: The view along the sheltered facade.

Opposite right: Exposed aggregate panels beneath the windows and gargoyle rain spouts on each floor.

The Great Library at the University of East Africa (now the University of Nairobi) was an icon of 1960s African modernism—with all of the contradictions that the movement entailed. Kenya had won its independence from Britain in 1963, but the overhaul of government and institutions brought with it many opportunities for British architects and engineers. At a moment when architecture was being seized upon as an important means of expressing national identity, the Great Library at what was still the university's Royal College had been designed by an Old Etonian. The resulting building was in a sort of tropical London modernism, with the bold concrete beams, slabs and columns of grey northern Europe contorted into new forms under the hot sun and fierce storm clouds of East Africa.

The Great Library was intended to play a key role in the independent country, housing a national collection of half a million books. The building had to be a landmark—albeit one on a strict budget—and the British architect Anthony M Chitty, a former member of Berthold Lubetkin's partnership Tecton, was commissioned to design it. Working with Ove Arup, Chitty came up with a fairly conventional rectangular building with a reinforced concrete column-and-beam frame and slab floors. The Kenyan climate, however, demanded some unconventional thinking.

The first problem was how to keep out the sun. The roof, which took the form of a concrete slab concertinaed into a zigzag, projected 15 feet out from the facade, but this only shaded the upper levels. Beneath the roof, therefore, another vast shading system was devised, comprising a screen of in-situ concrete brise-soleil. These columns stood forwards from the main facade and were linked, at first-floor level, by a deep zigzag beam, echoing the folded roof. Halfway up the building, a series of 12-foot-deep concrete shelves were inserted between the columns to shield the lower storeys further.

After the sun, however, came the rain—the intensity of tropical storms in Kenya meant that gutters and enclosed downpipes were avoided as much as possible. Instead, the folded roof acted as its own gutter, falling slightly to one end where the water was thrown off by a series of precast gargoyles. Further gargoyles were placed at the head of the open downpipes on the east side of the building.

Surface finishes throughout were chosen on the grounds of economy and low maintenance, but were "nevertheless extremely effective". The vertical brise-soleil had a facing of chunks of Kenya marble—"a white, sparkling, quartz-like stone"—set in white cement, while another local stone, the dark grey "black trap", was used elsewhere as large exposed aggregate.

In its materials and context, as well as its timing, the Great Library was undeniably an African building. But it is easy to see something of the Englishman abroad—has sunscreen ever come in a higher factor than 12-foot-deep concrete?

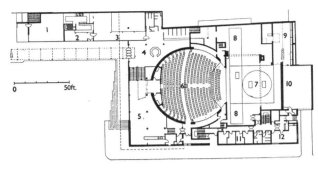

Above: Ground floor plan. The cafe, bar and restaurant are marked 1, 2 and 3 in the wing to the top left.

Left: The auditorium, showing stage lighting fixed to the concrete gallery edge.

Below: Board-marked concrete and metallic decoration in the foyer.

Nottingham Playhouse
Nottingham, UK
Peter Moro

Issue 63, Winter 1964

The theatre from the entrance
forecourt. The drum of the auditorium,
in board-marked concrete, rises behind
the glazed screens of the foyers.

Nottingham Playhouse was the quintessential modern theatre. The city's Repertory Company had benefited from public subsidy since the late 1940s, which meant that the brief for its new home called for less pomp and more civic-mindedness than traditional theatre design.[17] Peter Moro, the co-designer of the Royal Festival Hall, took on the role of architect and put in a performance of restrained classiness.

From the outside, the Playhouse was inherently public-spirited. The glazed facade revealed a restaurant, bar and cafe, all accessible from the street, with the circular concrete auditorium rising up behind. The foyer was equally inviting, designed as a continuation of the external paving, with the flagstones carried through without a break.

The interior treatment was defined by the drum of the auditorium, which curved round in "a great sweep" of board-marked concrete at the back of the foyer. *Concrete Quarterly* noted that the concrete struck "a nice balance between the too careful and the too *brut*: it has just enough variations in texture and colour to be interesting without being disruptive, and never

appears crude".[18] The local aggregate was of a high quality, so a dry mix could be used, enhancing the imprint of the ply-backed boards. And the colour was never merely a flat grey: "In some parts it is tinged with buff tones, not unlike the colour found in Bath stone, whilst in others there are drifts of light silver, rather as one sees in weathered Portland stone."

But what really made the concrete shine was its interplay with other materials: "The foil of rough concrete to smooth glass, hard concrete to soft carpet, matt concrete to sparkling lights and—perhaps—primitive concrete to the sophisticated trappings of theatre-going." In this, Nottingham paved the way not only for Denys Lasdun's National Theatre but also for twenty-first-century playhouses such as Haworth Tompkins' Everyman in Liverpool.[19]

"Here, at last, is a building that manages to make use of 'natural' materials in a direct and simple manner without looking austere", concluded *Concrete Quarterly*. "Those who have never much liked concrete as finish might take a look at this theatre; those who like it anyway will be pleased to find one of the most satisfying examples so far in Britain."

Elephant House, London Zoo
London, UK
Hugh Casson

Issue 66, Autumn 1965

Above: The elephant side of the building. Slots in the wall allowed smaller visitors to see the animals.

Right: The pool in the elephant paddock seen from the roof. The shape was partly determined by the re-use of the sick-bay formwork.

Opposite: The timber roof structure, hanging low "like a labyrinth of branches".

At the height of Brutalism, it took an elephant house to show off concrete's lighter side. Hugh Casson's new enclosure for London Zoo's largest residents was all elephantine curves and ribbed, bush-hammered surfaces, like a wrinkled, leathery hide. This was concrete in the service of spectacle, showing off the Zoo's exotic stars to their best advantage.

The interior featured further deft touches, the timber roof structure hanging "low and dark over the public like a labyrinth of branches, with shafts of top light over the animals so that they are come upon as if in a jungle clearing".

But *Concrete Quarterly* was quick to point out that the building, and in particular its use of materials, was highly functional. After all, elephants made for very demanding clients.

> Externally curved plinths of dark blue brick and the ribbed concrete discourage the animals from marking the walls. Internally, the plan is curved for easy cleaning of the walls and to minimise the chance of damage to the mosaic [linings].[20]

The choice of structural material had another obvious advantage: "The building acts as a stockade—a vertical cantilever of reinforced concrete."

The vertical walls were cast in situ in three lifts and the ribbing was achieved by inserting wedge-shaped fillets into the timber formwork, which was then re-used "repeatedly". After striking, the concrete surfaces were "roughly hacked by one man using a hammer and bolster". This, it turns out, was not to replicate elephant skin, but rather was inspired by "the similarly treated piers of Twickenham Bridge designed by Maxwell Ayrton in the early thirties".

But regardless of Casson's intentions, it is the building's essential elephantness that has ensured its enduring popularity. "[It demonstrates] the creative force of concrete when handled with discernment", wrote the architect and planner Alfred Wood 20 years after it was built.[21] Casson had shown that robust concrete could be witty as well as aggressive—and (with the help of some 6-tonne pachyderms) could bring a smile to the public's face.

Dunelm House
Durham, UK
Architects Co-Partnership,
Ove Arup

Issue 69, Summer 1966

Above: Dunelm House seen from the approach road at the top of the site.

Right: View of the River Wear from one of the multi-level terraces.

Below: Externally, walls of board-marked lightweight concrete were used extensively for insulation.

Below right: Broad steps leading to the upper entrance, with Durham Cathedral in the background.

Right: The building seen from across the River Wear, with Ove Arup's Kingsgate footbridge in the foreground.

The expansion of Durham University in the 1960s gave Britain two of its finest concrete structures. First came Ove Arup's Kingsgate Bridge, a taut band of white slicing across the top of the city's dramatic river gorge, connecting the existing university with a potential development site on the opposite bank. Then came the development itself, a student centre called Dunelm House.

Designed by Architects Co-Partnership (ACP), Dunelm House appeared to erupt from the landscape. "The site is dramatic in the extreme", wrote *Concrete Quarterly*, "sloping steeply down the gorge-like bank of the River Wear in two directions—from east to west, and south to north."[22] The building closely followed the contours of the hillside, its cantilevered concrete volumes cascading down the bank like an immense rockfall. The sheer sense of mass, almost dragging the building into the river, was a brilliant counterpoint to the levity of Arup's bridge—the architectural critic Rowan Moore has argued that the two, along with the mighty Norman cathedral towering over the opposite bank, should be considered as a monumental ensemble, "exploring masonry's full range of mass and levitation".[23]

For *Concrete Quarterly*, Dunelm House was simply a very sophisticated, modern university building. The magazine was particularly impressed with the unity of the design, and how imaginatively it had integrated the various functions within its compact structure of in-situ reinforced concrete boxes:

Its size, apparently small from the top boundary, is more apparent from the bridge and the other side of the river, but even from here it is not really possible to appreciate the

amount of accommodation that has been tucked away into the hillside.

The layout, with its various levels and cantilevers, was easier to follow in section than plan and hinged around a main stairway with magnificent framed views of the cathedral. The stair "acts as a stepped spine", *Concrete Quarterly* explained, "descending from the main entrance at high level, with rooms off at each landing as it goes down, ending with the dance hall—the largest room in the building".

Much of the furniture was specially designed and built in, including the billiard table, which had a standard top fixed to a concrete pedestal. Most of the artificial lighting and all of the ventilation grilles were also incorporated into the structure. Robust concrete finishes were used throughout, even on the roof, which was covered in precast lapped tiles with an exposed aggregate finish of pink Shap granite.

Dunelm House currently faces an uncertain future. The university, keen once more to expand and provide new facilities, has been granted a certificate of immunity, which stops the building from being listed for five years, allowing it to be altered or—the university's preferred option—demolished. It is in danger of following that other concrete masterpiece by ACP and Arup, Brynmawr Rubber Factory, into the vanishing past.

Wexham Park Hospital
Slough, UK
Powell & Moya

Issue 71, Winter 1966

Above: The administration block seen from the centre of the entrance court.

Right: Exit from one of the garden courts, by way of steps between retaining walls of bush-hammered concrete.

Left: The administration block's entrance hall, with tapering board-marked columns and a dramatic faceted ceiling.

Below: Textured white concrete elements were contrasted with coffee-coloured rendering.

For most of us, the hospital is a place to be approached with awe and some trepidation. And if it is designed in a certain impersonal idiom, the total effect can reduce some people to mere shadows. All credit then, to the architects Powell and Moya, who have done the reverse, and produced a new hospital, stretching its limbs into the leafy green of Buckinghamshire, which makes you feel—if not exactly welcome—at least at home directly you pass through the gates. No white tiles and whiff of formaldehyde here....[24]

In 1966, Britain's hospitals were undergoing much-needed modernisation. Harold Wilson's new government boasted that it was spending £1.5 million a week to update facilities, and by the end of the year, work was underway on more than 130 hospitals. Along with the new universities, this represented perhaps the most profound reworking of a building type in 1960s Britain. And as with the new universities, two architects were proving especially prolific: Philip Powell and Hidalgo Moya.

Powell & Moya's 300-bed Wexham Park Hospital near Slough was to become the "most admired and imitated post-war hospital in Britain".[25] It was economical, with a quietly domestic air, but it was also, in its layout, somewhat radical. The main wards were arranged in low-rise L-shaped blocks with large windows overlooking courtyard gardens. This was in line with the latest ideas on hospital efficiency—"it has been calculated that the time taken for journeys is less [than in a multi-storey ward block], and delays waiting for and getting in and out of lifts are eliminated"—but it was also considered to be more human-centric, with patients able to have as much contact with the surrounding gardens as possible.

It is striking how similar the thinking behind these blocks was to many of the health "communities" proposed today, with flexibility, daylight and natural surroundings all considered essential. Moya saw the hospital as "a village or small town which can grow and where each sector, while being unmistakably part of the same organism, has its own individual character".

The 'sector' with the most character was undoubtedly the campus' one vertical element: the eight-storey administration tower. Designed by Paul Koralek and engineer Felix Samuely, the block was "all lightness, springing into the air like a fountain from four tapering columns". In the entrance hall, the columns appeared "to be cushioned by a 'quilting' of faceted in situ concrete"—a remarkable segmented ceiling that has been likened to a pineapple skin. The exposed concrete was cast against wrought softwood boards and left as it came from the forms. It was, *Concrete Quarterly* marvelled, "a fascinating study in the plasticity of concrete construction".

St Peter's Seminary
Glasgow, UK
Gillespie, Kidd & Coia

Issue 72, Spring 1967

Above: A corner of the convent—
"comparable to a comfortable hotel".

Above right: The seminary from
above, with a side chapel to the fore
and the River Clyde just visible in
the background.

Right: Looking towards the deeply
cantilevered library and classroom wing
from the entrance hall steps.

Below: The chapel, with access
balconies to the study-bedrooms
cantilevered over the central space.

Right: Looking towards the ground-floor
chapel, with study-bedrooms above.

Religious orders had strong tastes in the 1960s. Six years after Le Corbusier's Monastery of La Tourette opened, Gillespie, Kidd & Coia's St Peter's Seminary rose out of the misty banks of the Clyde like a cross between a brooding Highlands castle and a Glasgow housing estate. With its muscular volumes, coarse-aggregate facades and bare concrete surfaces, the debt to Le Corbusier was clear. *Concrete Quarterly* thought it "splendidly virile and rugged.... Its powerful structural expression and natural materials seem right for a community of young men searching for basic values in the shifting sands of current doctrine."[26]

The seminary consisted of three buildings: a main block containing the chapel, refectory and study-bedrooms; a classroom block; and a small two-storey convent. On all three, the external treatment was "suitably vigorous" for the rugged setting. The main block and convent were faced in precast panels with aggregate of large brown pebbles, while the in-situ concrete structure of the classroom block was left exposed with strong board markings. Internally, most of the in-situ concrete was left deliberately rough. "This seems right in this context", wrote *Concrete Quarterly*, "and one cannot help thinking that over-careful concrete would have destroyed the elemental character of the seminary as a whole."

St Peter's was certainly austere. However, the use of the brutalist idiom placed it emphatically in the modern world.

Concrete Quarterly noted that the layout subtly blurred the division between the spiritual and material. The main block welded the activities of worship and study, eating and sleeping into an integrated whole, with the bedrooms overlooking the central space between the refectory and chapel. "If we think that the training of priests is designed to remove them from the realities of the modern world, we are wrong", reasoned *Concrete Quarterly*. "These boys will be as much at home with the transistor as with the rosary—as much at home in a good modern building as in some ancient cloister." Likewise, the small convent was at ease with the comforts of the age. The bare concrete and pine interiors seemed "rich rather than ascetic", while the timber-lined bedrooms were "comparable with those of a comfortable hotel".

Ultimately, however, it would be the building's raw, elemental nature rather than its modernity that would endure. The seminary closed in 1980, and it quickly became an eerie ruin: overgrown, roofless and skeletal. *Concrete Quarterly* had described it as "growing out of the Scottish soil in a manner one could almost call earthy", and now it seemed to be returning. It has recently been revived by arts organisation NVA, which plans to preserve the remaining structure and turn it into an events space. "Our role is not to make people like it", NVA's Angus Farquhar has explained. "That would be the least interesting thing you could do."[27]

Liverpool Metropolitan Cathedral
Liverpool, UK
Frederick Gibberd

Issue 73, Summer 1967

Above: The Cathedral pictured just before completion.

Right: View from the nave into the simple circular baptistery.

Left: At night, with the coloured glass of the lantern glowing richly from within.

Below: Floor plan showing the innovative circular layout.

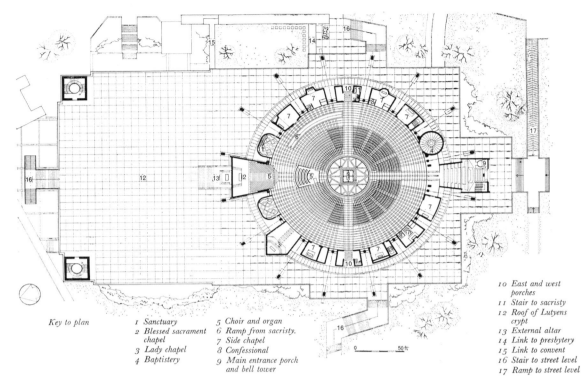

Key to plan

1 *Sanctuary*
2 *Blessed sacrament chapel*
3 *Lady chapel*
4 *Baptistery*
5 *Choir and organ*
6 *Ramp from sacristy.*
7 *Side chapel*
8 *Confessional*
9 *Main entrance porch and bell tower*
10 *East and west porches*
11 *Stair to sacristy*
12 *Roof of Lutyens crypt*
13 *External altar*
14 *Link to presbytery*
15 *Link to convent*
16 *Stair to street level*
17 *Ramp to street level*

0   50 ft

Two things are generally known about building cathedrals: it takes a very long time, and they're meant to last for centuries. On the first count, Frederick Gibberd's Metropolitan Cathedral of Christ the King upset the rulebook. Its structure of in-situ and precast concrete, and finishes of Portland stone, sheet aluminium and piercingly intense glass panels by John Piper and Patrick Reyntiens, took just four years to complete. But, unusually for a building of the fast-moving modern age, it was intended to last for at least 500 years.

The durability of the structure was a key consideration here. As *Concrete Quarterly* explained, "No one knows precisely of a material which has lasted 500 years in an atmosphere such as that of Liverpool, with its high winds, sea air and industrial atmosphere."[28] A frame of compressed concrete was chosen— after all, it had kept the Pantheon up for the best part of 2,000 years. The mix had as low a water-cement ratio as possible and limestone aggregate was specified for its elastic properties. The use of precast elements was also important: the 156 panels of latticed reinforced concrete and glass that comprised the central lantern could be easily removed for repair.

Of course, the other way to ensure longevity is to create a landmark that no one would want to knock down. Gibberd's cathedral was deliberately magnificent. From its position on the top of Brownlow Hill, the 70-foot-tall lantern "crowned" the city, just half a mile from its other crown, Giles Gilbert Scott's dark sandstone Anglican cathedral. "Even with the clamour of men at work (on a day before the consecration) and God not in, so to speak, until the following Saturday fortnight, there was—still—a sense of majesty in it all", wrote *Concrete Quarterly*.

The form of the building was driven by modern liturgical practice, with its emphasis on "audience participation rather than theatre at the end". The altar was placed at the centre, surrounded by a huge circular nave. This space was encircled by 16 reinforced concrete inclined ribs that swept up through the near-cylindrical lantern to the tips of the 70-foot-high prestressed concrete pinnacles. These in turn performed the triple role of completing the crown, adding height to the building and "dissolving the silhouette" into the misty Liverpool atmosphere.

Structure and architecture were seamlessly integrated. The ribs, which carried the weight of the 2,000-tonne lantern down to a framework of columns and buttresses, were one of the most impressive external features, seeming to soar up to the sky between the vast planes of the aluminium roof. Internally, too, the ribs served to divert the view upwards, to the massive exposed 78-foot-diameter ring beam and the jewel-like lantern beyond.

The only flaw that *Concrete Quarterly* could find was the finish of some of the internal concrete:

The surface is, in fact, so beautifully smooth that all irregularities of colour... are emphasised, even though this is carefully cast concrete. One could have wished for some roughening—bush hammering perhaps—of the surface texture to eradicate at least some of these superficial blemishes.

THE WORLD RECAST: 70 BUILDINGS FROM 70 YEARS OF *CONCRETE QUARTERLY*

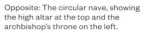

Opposite: The circular nave, showing the high altar at the top and the archbishop's throne on the left.

Left: Side view of the entrance porch and bell tower.

Right: Cover of the Summer 1967 issue.

Below left: Reinforced concrete buttresses covered with white mosaic cut across the chapels and porches.

Below right: Looking up into the lantern tower above the high altar.

Concrete Quarterly 73

CEMENT AND CONCRETE ASSOCIATION · APRIL—JUNE 1967 · PRICE FIVE SHILLINGS

1960–1969

Habitat '67
Montreal, Canada
Moshe Safdie

Issue 73, Summer 1967

Above: Looking down from a garden
into the heart of Habitat. It was "not
unlike a steep hillside town".

Right: View from the balcony garden
of one of the Habitat houses.

In 1967, Moshe Safdie reinvented the box.

At a time when the idea of system housebuilding was rapidly losing its novelty, the 29-year-old Canadian-Israeli architect showed that, actually, it hadn't gone far enough. His block of 158 flats for the 1967 Montreal Expo comprised concrete box-like elements made entirely in the factory, with kitchens, bathrooms, window frames, insulation and other fittings all installed on the assembly line. Each unit was 17 feet, 6 inches wide, 38 feet, 6 inches long and 10 feet high, and weighed between 70 and 90 tonnes. They were precast in steel moulds in a purpose-built facility next to the construction site, leaving the site team simply to lift the boxes into position by crane.

But Safdie's great trick was in turning one of the principal flaws of factory manufacture—the cold, boxy, repetitive geometry of the products—into an architectural virtue. The cubes were arranged into a complex stack connected by bolts and post-tensioning. This arrangement allowed for 15 different housing types, with gardens and terraces filling the voids. The seemingly arbitrary pattern of elements looked like a child's game—Safdie's practice cheerfully admitted that initial models had been built using Lego.

When *Concrete Quarterly* editor George Perkin visited the Expo in the summer of 1967, Safdie's "highly ingenious" development had already proved a magnet for the world's architectural press. But how, he wondered, did it actually look, and what would it be like to live in?

His initial impression was underwhelming—a simple vision of "uniform greyness".[29] But the pixelated form quickly cohered into something "intensely alive". The pattern of boxes, which was in fact strict and logical, had created a compact urban form with a variety of engaging indoor and outdoor spaces.

When you climb up into the suspended streets, wander into the spacious, free-planned houses—most on two levels and many with upper and lower garden balconies—and then look down over the stepped terraces and rooftops, it appears not unlike a town built into a steep hillside.

Housing was a problem that had thus far refused to be solved by the ingenuity of post-war architects and engineers, but in Habitat '67 Perkin saw an alternative to the looseness of suburbia and the rigid confinement of the multi-storey block.

One gets the impression of people being around, without anyone actually invading one's privacy. It would be difficult to imagine feeling cut off in such a place. It is varied, lively, unregimented and stimulating.

The project was not entirely successful. The original scheme of 358 flats had been scaled back by half in the face of spiralling costs, but even so the final bill was £4 million (about £430,000 a flat in today's money). *Concrete Quarterly* was quick to point out that, as a system of industrialised housing, the economics shouldn't be judged until it had been rolled out on a wider scale. But a more ambitious phase two, with banks of tent-like houses, was never built.

The idea of modular high-rise living was nonetheless a beguiling one. While some saw the repetitive concrete blocks of Habitat '67 as typically brutalist, others delighted in the concept of a building that could grow simply through the addition of more pre-designed units. Today, Habitat '67 has become a totem for the proponents of automated construction, while its stacked style has inspired a number of schemes in high-density cities such as Singapore and Hong Kong. Safdie's "Hanging Gardens of Montreal", it seems, had planted a seed.

Right: Interior showing the concrete hyperbolic paraboloid shells which make up the walls.

Opposite left: The exterior was clad in stainless-steel strips.

Opposite right: The curving concrete walls gave an "intentionally superhuman" scale to the interior.

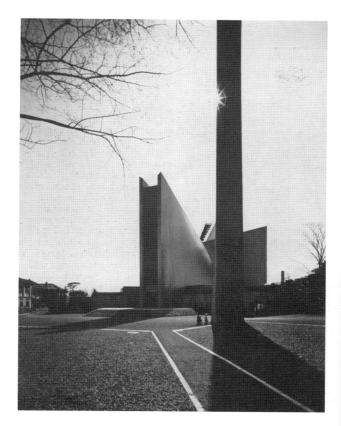

St Mary's Cathedral
Tokyo, Japan
Kenzo Tange

Issue 75, Winter 1967

Increasingly in the post-war period, Western eyes were turning to Japan, and in particular the work of Kenzo Tange. Working predominantly in concrete—both in situ and precast—Tange did much to develop a distinctively Japanese style in the medium. This grew out of the country's heritage of wooden construction, drawing on its pool of skilled carpenters to create meticulously crafted formwork; the concrete would then usually be used straight from the forms without further treatment.

The other characteristic of Japanese concrete architecture was its embrace of the material's inherent solidity, an understandable attraction given the region's long history of earthquakes and more immediate memories of the devastation of the Second World War. It is no coincidence that the first of Tange's buildings to come to wider international attention was the Hiroshima Peace Memorial Museum, 1956, built entirely of exposed reinforced concrete.

In October 1967, *Concrete Quarterly* joined a group of 114 British architects on a tour of the Far East to see how modern concrete architecture was transforming cities such as Hong Kong, Chandigarh and Bangkok. Tange's Roman Catholic cathedral in Tokyo was picked out as a highlight of the trip:

> The interior is breathtaking. The floor is diamond-shaped, from which plain concrete walls made up of eight vertical hyperbolic paraboloid shells soar to a great height to meet a cruciform roof with translucent natural lights. Tall narrow slit windows extend from roof to floor at the ends of the shells. The effect is, without exaggeration, exhilarating.[30]

The imposing, monolithic nature of raw concrete created an inherently religious experience:

> The concrete wall surfaces are almost completely unadorned and depend on subtle changes of plane and indirect lighting for their effect. In the centre of the cathedral the scale is intentionally superhuman.

The cathedral also showed concrete's uncanny ability to represent both modernity and something more medieval.

> It could be said that a characteristic of Gothic cathedrals is their peculiar spiritual quality achieved by soaring space, which does—in a way—transcend the material world around us. Tange has endeavoured to do the same thing in Tokyo cathedral but with modern concrete techniques.... There is the element of surprise, and of wonder.

National Center for Atmospheric Research Boulder, Colorado, US IM Pei

Issue 79, Winter 1968

Above: The bush-hammered finish of the concrete echoes the rocky landscape.

Right: View looking down into the entrance courtyard.

Concrete hoods give shade to the deeply recessed windows.

"Concrete is an artificial rock—but ultimately a rock", wrote the architect Artur Carulla in *Concrete Quarterly* in 2016.[31] Carulla, a partner at Allies and Morrison, was explaining the power of some concrete buildings that appear almost as outcrops in a natural, rocky landscape. The examples he cited included the 1994 Igualada Cemetery by Enric Miralles and Carme Pinós near Barcelona, and the 2003 Braga Stadium in Portugal by Eduardo Souto de Moura. But before either of these came the National Center for Atmospheric Research.

Designed by the Chinese-American architect IM Pei, the buildings of the National Center for Atmospheric Research stand 2,000 metres up in the Rocky Mountains outside Boulder, Colorado, and are striking for two reasons: their mysterious, hooded form, which gives them the impression of concrete sentinels guarding the mountains beyond; and their dramatic colour, "as pink as the rocky landscape which they regally survey".[32]

The finish was the result of extensive bush-hammering to the loadbearing in-situ concrete walls, which had brought out the colour of the locally quarried red limestone aggregate, creating the effect that these enigmatic, sculpted beings had simply risen from the mountain beds. In this, Pei had drawn inspiration from the Ancestral Puebloan people, who were native to the area and whose ancient Mesa Verde cliff dwellings appeared similarly to be carved out of the mountains.

The form of the buildings, meanwhile, had been driven by both aesthetic and function. The concrete hoods and louvres shaded all windows from the strong Colorado light, but the air of mystery was also entirely deliberate. "You cannot compete with the scale of the Rockies", Pei explained, "so we tried to make a building that was without the conventional scale you get from recognisable floor heights."

European visitors likened the building's impact to that of a medieval monastery on a rock in Catalonia or Tuscany. For *Concrete Quarterly*, it represented one of the most successful buildings yet by an architect whose confident handling of diverse typologies such as the Luce Memorial Chapel in Taiwan, 1963, and the Green Building at Massachusetts Institute of Technology, 1964, had given him "probably more experience of concrete than any other architect in the States". In an age where concrete had become synonymous with the urban realm, Pei showed that the material was just as at home in the wild.

1   Campbell, Betty, "Editorial", *Concrete Quarterly*, Issue 49, Summer 1961, p 1.

2   Calder, Barnabas, *Raw Concrete: The Beauty of Brutalism*, London: William Heinemann, 2016, p 5.

3   Campbell, "Editorial", Issue 49, p 1.

4   Campbell, Betty, "Editorial", *Concrete Quarterly*, Issue 53, Summer 1962, p 1.

5   Perkin, George, "Editorial", *Concrete Quarterly*, Issue 69, Summer 1966, p 1.

6   Perkin, George, "Concrete Murals", *Concrete Quarterly*, Issue 57, Summer 1963, p 19.

7   "The Revelation of Brazilian Architecture", *Concrete Quarterly*, Issue 18, Summer 1953, p 4.

8   "The Revelation of Brazilian Architecture", p 3.

9   "The Revelation of Brazilian Architecture", p 3.

10 "Brazil, Venezuela and Mexico: Notes on a tour organized by the Cement and Concrete Association in January–February this year", *Concrete Quarterly*, Issue 45, Summer 1960, pp 2–28. All subsequent quotations in this section are from this piece.

11 "Italy", *Concrete Quarterly*, Issue 25, 1955, p 10.

12 "The Pirelli building, Milan", *Concrete Quarterly*, Issue 51, Winter 1961, pp 18–25.

13 Forty, Adrian, *Concrete and Culture: A Material History*, London: Reaktion Books, 2012, p 181.

14 Perkin, George, "Le Corbusier's monastery of La Tourette", *Concrete Quarterly*, Issue 53, Summer 1962, pp 14–19. All subsequent quotations in this section are from this piece.

15 Franck, Nicolette, "Exploding Universities Build in Concrete", *Concrete Quarterly*, Issue 54, Autumn 1962, p 12.

16 Franck, "Exploding Universities Build in Concrete", p 12.

17 Fair, Alistair, "Building of the Month: Nottingham Playhouse", *The Twentieth Century Society* website, March 2009, https://c20society.org.uk/botm/nottingham-playhouse.

18 "High quality in situ concrete at The Nottingham Playhouse", *Concrete Quarterly*, Issue 63, Winter 1964, pp 2–5. All subsequent quotations in this section are from this piece.

19 See *Concrete Quarterly*, Issues 122 and 248, for respective discussions of the National Theatre and Everyman buildings.

20 "Concrete elephant house", *Concrete Quarterly*, Issue 66, Autumn 1965, pp 21–25. All subsequent quotations in this section are from this piece.

21 Wood, Alfred, "1965–75: Discovering the Environment", *Concrete Quarterly*, Issue 144, Spring 1985, p 31.

22 "Dunelm House – University of Durham", *Concrete Quarterly*, Issue 69, Summer 1966, pp 29–32. All subsequent references are from pp 29–32 of this feature unless otherwise stated.

23   Moore, Rowan, "Save Dunelm House from the
        Wrecking Ball", *The Observer*, 12 February 2017,
        www.theguardian.com/artanddesign/2017/feb/12/
        durham-university-dunelm-house-threat-of-
        demolition-brutalism.

24   "Low-rise hospital", *Concrete Quarterly*, Issue 71,
        Winter 1966, pp 10–17. All subsequent quotations in
        this section are from this piece.

25   Harwood, Elain, *Space, Hope and Brutalism: English
        Architecture 1945–1975*, New Haven, CT: Yale
        University Press, 2016, p 286.

26   "Scottish Seminary: St. Peter's College, Cardross",
        Concrete Quarterly, Issue 72, Spring 1967, pp 16–23.
        All subsequent quotations in this section are from
        this piece.

27   McVeigh, Tracy, "Scotland's Creepiest Building in £10m
        Restoration Scheme", *The Observer*, 18 September
        2011, www.theguardian.com/artanddesign/2011/
        sep/18/st-peters-seminary-cardross-architecture-
        modernism-heritage-restoration.

28   "Liverpool's concrete crown: The Metropolitan
        Cathedral of Christ the King", *Concrete Quarterly*,
        Issue 73, Summer 1967, pp 3–9. All subsequent
        quotations in this section are from this piece.

29   Perkin, George, "Expo Concrete", *Concrete Quarterly*,
        Issue 73, Summer 1967, pp 26–33. All subsequent
        quotations in this section are from this piece.

30   Perkin, George, "Far East Journey", *Concrete
        Quarterly*, Issue 75, Winter 1967, pp 28–32. All
        subsequent quotations in this section are from
        this piece.

31   Carulla, Artur, "Lasting Impression", *Concrete
        Quarterly*, Issue 258, Winter 2016, p 19.

32   "National Centre for Atmospheric Research",
        Concrete Quarterly, Issue 79, Winter 1968, pp 2–5.
        All subsequent quotations in this section are from
        this piece.

1970–1979

Clifton Cathedral
Bristol, UK
Percy Thomas Partnership,
Felix J Samuely & Partners
Issue 100, Spring 1974

And then the doubts set in. By the start of the 1970s, there was a growing sense that modern didn't always mean better. The collapse of the Ronan Point tower block in a gas explosion in 1968 had shattered many of the utopian dreams surrounding high-rise living and system building. There was also, as town planner Alfred Wood recalled a decade later, a growing resentment of

> the new motorways slicing through cherished countryside [and] slum-clearance schemes bulldozing companionable Coronation Streets... and decanting the former occupants into new prize-winning and sterile local-authority estates on the edge of town.[1]

Things came to a head in 1973 when the Organization of Arab Petroleum Exporting Countries (OPEC) proclaimed an oil embargo. If cheap energy had been the technological advance that unleashed the flowering of bold, expressive architecture in the previous decade, then the quadrupling of oil prices by OPEC demanded an equally radical rethink of the way we built—and even whether building was always the answer.[2] As Bryan Jefferson, the former president of the Royal Institute of British Architects, wrote in *Concrete Quarterly*: "By the mid-1970s many of us had a distinct feeling that the party was over."[3]

Like its readers, *Concrete Quarterly* too began to think smaller. In 1972, after years of reporting on the birth of motorways, it published a nine-page article on foot streets—"the reasons are obvious, with world-wide concern over the environment in general and pollution in particular"[4]—and began to champion low-rise, small-scale housing as "the very nerve centre of the environment".[5] In 1979, it devoted a whole issue to gardens.[6]

To many people, concrete was part of the problem. "It doesn't need great insight or perspicacity to see that concrete, per se, is now the fashionable scapegoat for all manner of social ills from vandalism and litter-throwing to sheer bad planning and design", wrote editor George Perkin in *Concrete Quarterly*'s 100th issue. "To be honest, it is true that much of this chat springs from poor concrete finishes, unsightly stains and streaks and bad weathering."[7]

The irony is that the 1970s were, in fact, a great age of concrete architecture. Many of the techniques developed over the previous decade were now raised to new levels of expertise: the board-marking on the

National Theatre was virtually flawless, while on the Côte d'Azur Jacques Couëlle was creating improbably organic forms with sprayed concrete. It was still the chosen material for much religious architecture, and it made Sydney's magnificent new opera house stand up. The problem was not so much with concrete, *Concrete Quarterly* reasoned, but with a press that fed the public a diet of architectural disasters.[8]

In many ways, concrete was precisely the material for the age. With people suddenly viewing energy as a precious resource and growing slightly neurotic about technology's ability to solve all of its problems, concrete's primitive qualities were both practical and reassuring—high levels of insulation and big solid walls were almost as desirable as the latest colour television sets.

The wild days were over; now concrete was becoming a responsible citizen.

Senior Combination Room, Downing College
Cambridge, UK
Howell, Killick, Partridge & Amis,
David Powell and Partners

Issue 86, Autumn 1970

Above: Interior view showing the
column and beam structure supporting
the central precast concrete lantern.

Right: The Combination Room
with the 1818 Dining Hall by William
Wilkins alongside.

Opposite: The four-columned portico
and broken pediment give a respectful
nod to the Wilkins Dining Hall.

The colleges of Oxford and Cambridge were some of architecture's most adventurous clients during the 1960s and 70s—and few did more to further the cause of concrete. Faced with the need to grow and modernise, they looked to international rivals, particularly Yale and Harvard, to see what modern university buildings should look like. Arne Jacobsen set down an early marker with his design for the new St Catherine's College in Oxford—a traditional quad-based campus distilled into imposing planes of precast concrete and glass. There followed Sheppard Robson's Churchill College, Cambridge; Chamberlin, Powell and Bon's New Hall, Cambridge; and Powell & Moya's Wolfson College, Oxford, as well as a string of striking garden buildings by Philip Dowson of Arup Associates.

One of the most prolific of the Oxbridge architects of the period was Howell, Killick, Partridge and Amis (HKPA). In Oxford, HKPA was responsible for the Hilda Besse building at St Antony's College and the reconstruction of much of St Anne's, developing and refining a tough language of projecting, faceted precast concrete panels. It had no intention of tiptoeing around the hushed cloisters: in Cambridge, it even dropped the brutalist University Centre onto a riverside meadow next to one of the city's most bucolic pubs.

But concrete architecture didn't need to scare the punters. The Senior Combination Room at Downing College is a work on a smaller scale and shows a nimbler touch. The 1970 Concrete Society Award judges even described it as witty.[9] The building, essentially a garden pavilion for the college fellows, is closely related to the concrete post-and-beam structures that were rising on quads elsewhere in the city. But with its four-columned portico and broken pediment, it gives a respectful nod to its elders too—notably William Wilkins' early nineteenth-century dining hall next door.

There is a lightness to it: the structure appears open, with an inner and outer square of precast concrete columns to break the line of the external enclosure, while a series of long cantilevered brackets support a central roof lantern. The precast concrete is a refined, high-quality mix of Skye marble and white cement, with the columns and beams made three inches oversized so that they could be ground down and finished with an acid wash. This sharp aesthetic is complemented by Portland stone panelling and expanses of glass.

There was also a darker note. The exaggerated junctions between the external posts and beams seemed to echo the timber construction of a gibbet. Amid all the light and refinement, HKPA couldn't resist a moment of gallows humour.

Taranto Cathedral
Puglia, Italy
Gio Ponti

Issue 91, Winter 1971

Top: View from the south-east, showing the two perforated precast concrete facades.

Above right: The structure was expressed internally with projecting winged columns which reduced the spans of the beams.

Right: The rear facade of the cathedral. Offices and priests' residences overlook the courtyard cloister.

Above: Choir stalls.

Right: The south facade. The freestanding structures over the doorways were designed to be covered with creepers.

In 1971, *Concrete Quarterly* scored a major coup when the legendary Italian architect Gio Ponti agreed to write a ten-page article on his recently completed Great Mother of God Co-Cathedral in Taranto, southern Italy. Being the hands-on sort, he also offered to design and lay out the pages. For Ponti, it was an opportunity to explain the role of symbolism in his religious work, as well as to wax lyrically about how rapturously the cathedral had been received. At the consecration, he related,

> Something happened that perhaps has no precedent in the history of architecture: the architecture itself was given unexpected and prolonged applause—in the presence of its architect—from all the people pressed into the cathedral.[10]

The clapping, he felt it his journalistic duty to report, "began repeatedly and went on for long moments at a time without stopping".

Whether or not this account is entirely objective, it is hard to imagine such a response to Ponti's earlier work, the sleek, super-cool Pirelli Tower in Milan. But Taranto Cathedral was a different beast entirely—one that channelled the spirit of the Gothic as much as the modern age. For such a project, Ponti wrote,

> the very first thoughts must be about intensity and expressive force of religious feeling, rather than about... architectural criteria such as proportion, relationship of volumes and spaces, design etc.

The use of symbolism was pronounced, particularly in the two magnificent architectural set pieces: the entrance facade overlooking the main steps and the higher perforated facade behind, which towered over the presbytery. The entrance was punctured by tall windows, which served the purpose of anticipating the cathedral nave and receiving the congregation. The higher facade, meanwhile, was also an entrance, symbolically speaking. The ornate pattern of rectangular and hexagonal openings was a

> door to the skies, and means that if the Creator is everywhere, and He is in the interior of the Church, He is also in the immense space of the skies.

This was not the mysterious, austere intensity of Le Corbusier's Monastery of La Tourette, but an overt religious language intended to communicate directly to the "simple-hearted expectations" of ordinary believers.

The cathedral was clad in plaster but the structure was built entirely from in-situ reinforced concrete. Ponti had come to see concrete not simply as a new language in architecture but as a gateway to a new way of thinking. Like Oscar Niemeyer, whose free and expressive forms he greatly admired, he claimed to have intuition about the material and what it could do.[11] "Without the existence of concrete", he wrote, "not only could this architectural design never have been realized, it could not even have been thought of, in that it was only possible to imagine it in relation to the possibilities offered by concrete."

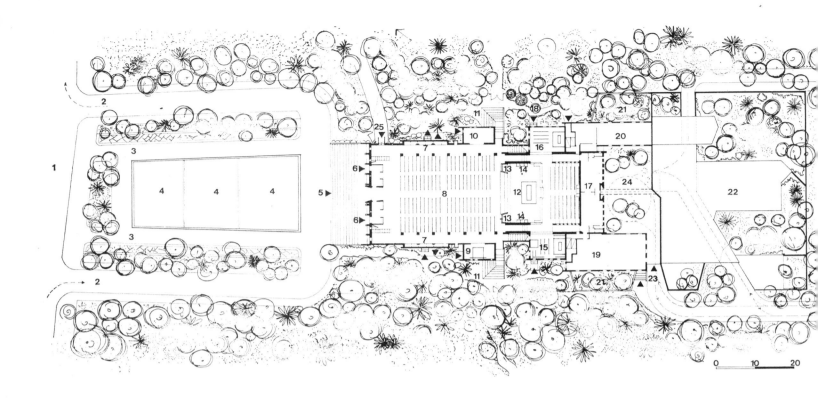

Plan of the cathedral, indicating the processional way [3], entrance steps [5], confessionals [7], nave [8], baptistery [9], seamen's chapel [10], altar [12], Chapel of the Madonna del Mantello [15], Chapel of the Sacrament [16], sacristy with choir above [17] and priests' offices and residences [19].

Above: Ponti also painted the Annunciation.

Left: The architect wanted the whole cathedral to be surrounded by greenery.

Various internal views. Walls were pure white, while floors were of green ceramic tiles.

Port la Galère
Provence, France
Jacques Couëlle

Issue 91, Winter 1971

Views of the village looking
west across the beach. The
houses achieved "a remarkable
degree of organic unity with the
rocky landscape".

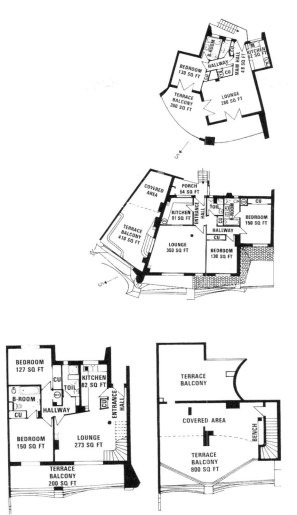

Typical layouts of the different house types.

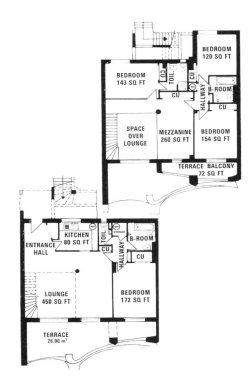

Strange things were afoot on the Côte d'Azur in the early 1970s. First, a new village appeared in the rocky hills behind Cannes; and then another, cascading down a steep hill to the Mediterranean. What was striking about both of these developments was that there was not, as *Concrete Quarterly* editor George Perkin observed, a straight line or rectangle to be found on either of them: "All is sculpture, some houses look like caves."[12] It was as if the ghost of Gaudí had taken a holiday at the seaside.

The two villages—Castellaras-le-Neuf and Port la Galère— were the work of the maverick Marseillais Jacques Couëlle. Architect is perhaps too narrow a term for Couëlle. "He seems to have been in his time a poet, visionary, sculptor, artist, biologist, archaeologist, philosopher..." wrote Perkin. The French writer Armand Lanoux, a friend of Couëlle, wrote of him:

> He patented invention after invention: concrete made on the analogy of living cells, torsion beams that were the talk of all architectural magazines, electrical conductors based on the nervous system, walls and floors whose inspiration was the whale's skin. He was a sorcerer, himself bewitched by too vast a universe.[13]

Built when Couëlle was in his late 60s, the two Mediterranean villages are the most complete expressions of his restless mind. The houses were the very essence of organic architecture— curving, bending and arching as if shaped by the forces of nature. "My houses are living beings", Couëlle had written, "They have a

nervous system, a stomach, intestines, a heart. They are built like madreporic sponges." In another episode in his eventful life, he had founded the Centre for Research in Natural Studies in Paris to study "the lessons of the sponges".

Perkin visited Port la Galère in the summer of 1971 and was immediately impressed:

> Perhaps nobody but Jacques Couëlle, as deeply rooted in the soil of the Midi as the red rocks and the pines which grow out of it, could have designed anything so unmistakably Mediterranean without making it purely imitative or sentimentalized. It is neither of these things. With its rock-like clusters of houses it is obviously one man's personal vision and a brilliant conception at that.

This was the heyday of package tourism all along Europe's Mediterranean coastline, and the south of France had not been spared the tide of bland resorts. "It is terrible to see what has happened to the Côte d'Azur since the war", wrote Perkin, "indiscriminate 'campings', cafeterias and—more recently— mammoth though lucrative apartment blocks of almost shocking brutality." Port la Galère seemed to offer a way forward: houses of modern materials geared to modern needs, which at the same time achieved a "remarkable degree of organic unity with the landscape" and preserved the spirit of this part of the Côte.

Not that this was an ordinary tourist development, aimed as it was at well-heeled Parisians, Londoners and New Yorkers in

Below: Deep balcony terraces defined the external appearance of the houses.

Right: View looking west across the bay.

Below right: Steps down to the harbour.

Opposite: Some of the houses were built up on the cliff edge.

search of Provençal sun and a private beach. "At the entrance to the village at the top of the hill there is a road barrier with a guard in a box", noted Perkin. "The casual visitor is put through a gruelling cross-examination and very likely refused entrance." The name *Concrete Quarterly* must have travelled far in those days, as our man was eventually let through. Once inside, Perkin could examine at first hand Couëlle's signature architectural style, and the secret behind his "inhabitable sculptures".

The first revelation was that, in plan, all of the buildings were rectilinear, with core walls of concrete blockwork. The sculptured arcades, terraces, balconies and galleries that made up the external expression were in fact a type of cladding: the block walls were covered with mesh, followed by sprayed concrete and a rendering of pigmented white cement to produce the light terracotta and sand-coloured finishes. Lanoux gave a vivid account of Couëlle's working method, which involved standing on site with a megaphone, directing operations, "digging with a pneumatic drill into the rough-hewn rock and adding the missing volumes with a cement gun that vaporizes a dry-mixed concrete".

To some minds such a treatment might have appeared superficial. This was, after all, an age in which any personal expression in architecture was viewed with suspicion. But Perkin felt the artifice was justified on practical as well as aesthetic grounds:

In this climate and with these views, outdoor living is at least as important as indoor, and the provision of cool terraces for sitting out, with barbecues and their chimneys, and of deeply shaded rooms is really the essence of life here.

The play of light through the seemingly random openings, which were filled with coloured glass like "multi-coloured goblets", was also carefully orchestrated—part of Couëlle's philosophy of bringing the landscape into the house.

You might not be surprised to learn that there was a lot more to Couëlle's philosophy of architecture—"all sorts of dark broodings about Freud and womb-like structures and protection"—but Perkin concluded that this was not the time or place to elaborate on them. "No doubt, from a cursory glance at the pictures, you will get the general idea...."

Left: The training vessel *Dewaratji* anchored off Sydney Opera House during the bicentenary celebrations of Captain Cook's landing in Australia.

Below: The shell structures being clad with precast concrete panels faced with ceramic tiles.

Sydney Opera House
New South Wales, Australia
Jørn Utzon; Hall, Todd and Littlemore;
Ove Arup and Partners

Issue 99, Winter 1973

Right: Aerial view of the shells.

Opposite: "Sometimes like the wide open jaws of a whale".

The famous contours of Sydney Opera House are clad in over one million ceramic tiles. But beneath those tiles lie about 15 years' worth of sleepless nights. The concrete structure of the shell-like roof was a remarkable feat of engineering by an Arup team led by Jack Zunz—all the more so because when architect Jørn Utzon designed it, he had no idea whether it could be built. It was "the stuff of dreams", wrote Zunz, and although he didn't say it explicitly, the implication was that it was an engineer's worst nightmare:

> I don't think that [Utzon] ever really understood the complexity of the problems he was creating. Nor do I believe that he understood the problem-solving process which ensued when new technology had to be developed or even when existing technology had to be adapted for new and untried forms.[14]

The roof of the Sydney Opera House is remarkable for a number of reasons. First, it is the most recognisable silhouette created in the twentieth century. For Zunz, it was a work of art "with a capital A". For *Concrete Quarterly* it was already beyond doubt that it would go down as "the building of the century".

The second remarkable thing about the roof is how completely impractical it is. When Utzon resigned from the project in 1966, the interior still had to be designed, and the new architects, Hall, Todd and Littlemore, found to their horror that the accommodation requirements could barely fit beneath the iconic shells. For *Concrete Quarterly* in 1973, tiring perhaps of the modern age's relentless pragmatism, this was a fact to be revelled in:

The building is, if you like, a monumental denial of the modern creed that form should follow function... It is perhaps fascinating for some to speculate that the inside has very little to do with the outside. But so what?

Arguably the most remarkable thing about the roof of the Sydney Opera House, however, is that immense concrete structure. The great half-shells were up to 55 metres high and 57 metres wide, and appeared in elevation as a triangular segment of a circle with a radius of 75 metres. Part of the Arup team's genius was in conceiving a practical construction method for these immense, complex shapes by reducing them, as far as possible, to a number of similar elements.

The main shells were comprised of precast concrete ribs made from 4.6-metre segments, while the side shells were a series of in-situ concrete arches with precast beams. The shells were covered with 4,000 chevron-shaped precast concrete panels, each one reinforced with steel mesh and curved to follow the contours of the sphere. Only the joints in the panels, which coincided with the main shell ribs, gave any indication of the structure within. Everything else was discreetly concealed— like Zunz's nightmares—by the tiles.

"It is interesting to speculate whether Utzon would have had the same kind of vision if he had also had the sort of mind capable of immediately grasping the technical implications", wondered *Concrete Quarterly*. "Would the vision not, perhaps, have been watered down to meet what he imagined to be technically possible?"

Clifton Cathedral
Bristol, UK
Percy Thomas Partnership,
Felix J Samuely & Partners

Issue 100, Spring 1974

Above: The concrete flèche with
two bells incorporated at the base
of the cross.

Above right: The sanctuary and nave
viewed from the upper gallery. The
white concrete finishes are further
enhanced by top lighting.

Right: One of the Stations of the Cross,
which William Mitchell carved into
the concrete panels as they set.

Above: The Blessed Sacrament Chapel, showing the fine quality and regular board markings of the in-situ white concrete walls.

At Clifton Cathedral, George Perkin had, if not a revelation, then at least a moment of faith restored.

> At a time when I thought that I was going off boardmarked in-situ concrete forever, I am suddenly disconcerted by this fine example of a wholly in-situ white concrete interior which bears the imprint of redwood boards from Russia.... Never have I liked this technique so well since we first visited the Paris Unesco building back in the late 50s.[15]

The concrete was the work of John Laing Construction and structural engineer Felix Samuely, working to a design by Percy Thomas Partnership. The exposed walls were all cast in situ using detailed formwork of thin timber boards fixed onto plywood sheets. White cement gave a very light finish, which reflected the daylight drawn in through the roof's spire-like funnel. This play of light reminded Perkin of Kenzo Tange's St Mary's Cathedral in Tokyo in the way that it "inspired feelings of almost tangible spiritual reality". The skilful handling of indirect natural light, he concluded, was "surely the most effective way of invoking spiritual atmosphere".

Light is, however, nothing without space, which meant that Samuely had to devise a structural system with as few intermediate columns as possible. The basic form was of three hexagons stacked on top of each other. Walls and beams were of 18-inch-thick reinforced concrete, and the roof structure expressed as deep triangulated coffers. A beam arrangement in the shape of a star supported the hexagonal roof above the sanctuary. The whole structure affected an air of apparent simplicity which was integral to the overall sense of "serenity and delight".

Concrete was put to every use imaginable at Clifton. Artist William Mitchell carved the Stations of the Cross into the walls, and later recalled that he had only 90 minutes to work on each panel before it set.[16] Externally, the insulated in-situ walls were clad in large precast concrete panels with an exposed aggregate finish of Aberdeen granite, the pinkish brown colour echoing the surrounding buildings of Bath and Brandon stone.

Clifton Cathedral was, Perkin concluded, the perfect project with which to celebrate the magazine's century. It was, after all, "a British building which, from the concrete and architectural points of view, stands out from all our hundred issues".

1970–1979

Sir Thomas White Building,
St John's College
Oxford, UK
Arup Associates

Issue 110, Autumn 1976

Above: View looking towards
the entrance.

Above right: Looking towards the
entrance and porter's lodge, with
the old buildings on the left.

Right: Generous windows were an
important element of the design of
the study-bedrooms. Lattice screens
were fitted to offer privacy.

Opposite: View across the lawns to
the Middle Common Room pavilion.

In 1970s Oxbridge, the H-frames of Philip Dowson were becoming as ubiquitous as future Cabinet ministers. As its name suggests, the H-frame was a structure of vertical and horizontal elements, and Arup Associates' Dowson had made it his trademark. On a series of student buildings, beginning at Somerville College in Oxford and Corpus Christi in Cambridge, he had used the device as a projecting frame set forward from the building envelope, essentially turning skin and structure inside out. Not only did this add interest to the facades, it also lent a degree of privacy to the rooms within, which meant, perhaps counter-intuitively, that they could be glazed from floor to ceiling.

By the time he designed the Sir Thomas White Building, Dowson had been honing the system for over a decade. Now, with one of the wealthiest Oxford colleges as his client, he took the opportunity to perfect it, lavishing the block of study-bedrooms with a frame "rich in architectural pleasures".[17]

The richest of these pleasures was the high-quality white precast concrete, which was made from grey limestone aggregate and white cement and then bush-hammered. In a 1981 interview, Dowson told *Concrete Quarterly* that he viewed in-situ and precast concrete as two totally different materials, and the contrast between this highly controlled effect and, for example,

the rough, imprecise material he used on the IBM Headquarters in Johannesburg is stark.[18]

The frame was finely detailed, creating "an overall texture of great intricacy and depth... which stops short of being over-elaborate". As at the earlier Leckhampton House at Corpus Christi, the edges of each frame were sliced off to create eight-sided window openings, while the junctions between the standardised elements were exaggerated to show the method of construction. Latticed screens behind the double-glazing added another layer of interest.

While Dowson's expressed structure may have given the appearance of a hard outer shell, it actually made the building more permeable, dissolving the distinction between outside and inside space. The frame acted as a colonnade, linking the block into the circulation of the college and "emphasising the relationship of the new to the existing".

The week before *Concrete Quarterly*'s 1981 interview, Dowson had spent a night in one of the Sir Thomas White Building's rooms, giving him pause to reflect on the design. "What I tried to do in those college buildings was to create a sense of generosity and enclosure within the larger framework of the college, and to preserve above all a domestic scale", he told the magazine. "I would do the same again."[19]

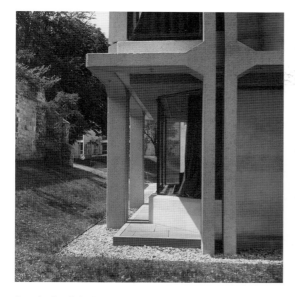

Opposite: Detail showing the articulation of the precast elements.

Above: The eastern corner showing the window of the Middle Common Room.

Right: A corner of the Middle Common Room.

Below: The concrete contained a grey limestone aggregate and white cement and was bush-hammered.

National Theatre
London, UK
Denys Lasdun and Partners,
Flint & Neill

Issue 112, Spring 1977

Above: The fan-shaped auditorium of
the Olivier, the largest of the National's
three theatres.

Right: Restaurant chairs were of
scarlet upholstery to offset the grey
concrete walls.

Left: "Never has concrete been so effectively illuminated as here."

Above: "Like a rockery waiting to be planted."

Architecture doesn't always fit neatly into decades. And so it is that the greatest concrete building of the 1960s was actually completed in 1976.

Along with Sydney Opera House, London's National Theatre was the most protracted building story of the 1970s. Its architect, Denys Lasdun, had been appointed back in 1963, when the plan also involved a neighbouring opera house, and the budget for the theatre was set at £2.3 million (about £28 million in 2017). From there, things quickly got horribly complicated. The scheme's main backer, the London County Council, disbanded in 1965, and Lasdun found himself working for a variety of competing interests, including a "Building Committee" chaired by Laurence Olivier and featuring luminaries of contemporary British theatre such as Peter Hall and Peter Brooke: a dream team for a production of *King Lear*, less so for a multimillion-pound architectural project. Debates dragged on for months over what form the main stage should take, and even how many auditoriums should be built, while relations with Lasdun became increasingly acrimonious.[20] Costs steadily escalated, and by 1966 the theatre alone was predicted to come in at £7.5 million (£91 million); the opera house was quietly dropped.

Work eventually started on site in 1969 but if anything, its problems were about to get worse. The London property boom of the late 1960s had placed skilled labour at a premium and the project was bedevilled by strikes. Then the 1973 energy crisis hit: the massive energy demands of a project on this scale were crippling as inflation shot up to over 20 per cent.[21] The National Theatre eventually opened three years later, at a cost of £16 million (£194 million)—seven times the original budget. But perhaps it was a miracle that it had opened at all.

By early 1977, the notoriety of this story had rather upstaged the building itself. But the fact was that London now had a magnificent public theatre—a third cultural jewel on the South Bank to go with the Royal Festival Hall and the South Bank Arts Centre. It was also an emphatically concrete building, one for which Lasdun had abandoned his usual, precisely controlled precast approach for impeccable board-marked in-situ concrete inside and out. This was the story that *Concrete Quarterly* wanted to tell when it visited for the first time that winter.

On entering, George Perkin immediately found that this was the sort of building you approached in hushed tones.

> Why, [my colleague] said, were we whispering, as if we were in church. Perhaps because there is indeed something noble and cathedral-like about those sudden soaring spaces and tall slender columns shooting up past the foyer galleries to the gridded ceiling above.[22]

Not that everyone was so moved by the grandeur of the space. "I am in a cave", Perkin overheard a fellow visitor remark.

Come the evening, however, the volume was raised, and the atmosphere transformed:

Opposite: Board-marked concrete
columns were lit from below by panels
set into the floor.

Right: View from the entrance porch
into the main foyers.

Below: Diagonal board-marked
concrete in the flanking walls of
the Lyttelton Theatre.

There is live music in the foyers, trumpeters and harpists and the young sitting on the floor all around... and the bars and buffets are full, and the spaces full of shadows and pools of light and people moving in mysterious silhouette against the backcloth of the Thames.

By traditional standards, the foyers were underlit, but this was an integral aspect of the architecture: "Never has concrete been so effectively illuminated as here", Perkin wrote. "The columns are mostly lit from below, the panels set flush in the floors, so that light is thrown upwards to reveal the full value of the grain in the boardmarking." It was almost as if Lasdun was lighting the concrete rather than the spaces.

Perkin did have reservations, particularly about the exposed-concrete exterior.

Outside, [board-marked concrete] is, to say the least, questionable, particularly in our damp grey climate... Concrete is a hard, grey, matt, rather primitive material. To show it off at its best it needs the contrast of soft, colourful, sparkling, rather sophisticated materials.... Internally it is quite easy to do this; externally it is much more difficult, unless it be with foliage.

The National Theatre was, one visitor observed, more like "a rockery waiting to be planted...."

It shows how widespread fears about the suitability of concrete as an external finish—and particularly the effects of weathering—had become by the late 1970s that even the editor of *Concrete Quarterly* was expressing unease at the sight of the National's grey facades. People were becoming restless with modernism. Even the awe-inspiring foyers didn't feel entirely in keeping with the spirit of the age. Lasdun disliked colour, decoration and what he called "costume jewellery" on buildings, and stated that he never wanted the National Theatre to be a "flossy hotel". Even so, Perkin couldn't help but wonder "how it would have been if just one concession to the ornamental traditions of theatre going had been permitted". He would have settled for a richly coloured carpet or two.

Much of the reaction to the National Theatre was the response of a 1970s audience to a 1960s building. But many of Perkin's initial impressions could equally apply today—even after the theatre has undergone two extensive refurbishments. During the day, there is, despite the cafes and shops, still an air of expectant hush unlike any other public space in London. And in the evening, the spaces are full of shadows and mysterious silhouettes against the backcloth of the Thames. A building that, as the historian Barnabas Calder put it, was built at precisely the wrong time for its architectural style has proved surprisingly timeless. [23]

Central Mosque
London, UK
Frederick Gibberd and Partners,
Posford Pavry and Partners

Issue 115, Winter 1977

Above: The mosque in its park setting.

Right: The copper dome is supported
on a reinforced concrete ring beam.

Above: The main congregation hall. The slab above is supported by four mushroom-head columns set back from the corners.

Right: The precast concrete units that formed the perimeter of the building each consist of two columns joined at the top by a four-centred arch of traditional Islamic profile.

In 1973 *Concrete Quarterly*, along with much of the rest of the world, had been blown away by the shape and silhouette of Sydney Opera House, "already as world famous as the Eiffel Tower, the Taj Mahal or the Pyramids", and wondered why Britain's modern architects had for so long ignored this aspect of design.[24] The most iconic shape on the London skyline was still Tower Bridge. Then came London Central Mosque—an Iranian style gold-clad dome and slender white minaret on the fringes of Regent's Park. While hardly a unique form in international terms, for 1970s London it was truly exotic.

The mosque was an unlikely marriage between the requirements of a strong religious tradition and the imagination of one of Britain's most illustrious post-war architects. Frederick Gibberd had cemented his reputation as a designer of modern religious buildings with Liverpool Metropolitan Cathedral, but here he took a more conservative approach, reflecting the client's desire for a traditional design with which worshippers would be familiar.[25]

What was less traditional was the method of construction. Gibberd and engineer Posford Pavry had developed a new method for building a dome. This involved covering the main hall with a flat reinforced concrete slab supported by mushroom-headed columns set back from the four corners—"like a table with inset legs".[26] The slab had a large circular hole in the centre with a reinforced concrete ring beam; this carried the light precast concrete segments that formed the drum beneath the dome. The dome itself consisted of eight tubular steel lattice frames, clad externally with gold alloy sheeting.

Precasting may have seemed like a surprisingly modern construction method for such a traditional architectural form, yet it lent itself well to the repetitive elements of Islamic design. The facades too were composed of identical precast units, each consisting of two columns joined at the top by a four-centred arch. These were cast with Derbyshire Spar aggregate and white cement, deep-ground for a smooth, pale finish, and infilled with glass or panels of white mosaic.

The Central Mosque was indisputably an Islamic building, but it was also modern and British. For *Concrete Quarterly*, it looked surprisingly at home in its park setting, "its gold shimmering dome and slim white minaret rising from a bower of dark summer green". London had its silhouette—not as grand as Sydney's maybe, but almost as dramatic amid the Nash terraces of Regent's Park.

Underhill House
Holme, West Yorkshire, UK
Arthur Quarmby

Issue 116, Spring 1978

Above: The top of the house was
covered in turf and used by a small
flock of sheep.

Right: A periscope from the kitchen
surveys the entrance.

Below: The pool and 'living garden' at night.

Right: The pool by day, lit by the central domed rooflight.

In 1978, *Concrete Quarterly* visited a grassy mound in the Peak District. On the face of it, these sheep-grazed berms didn't have much to do with concrete, or indeed architecture. But beneath the hill lay a highly original house—one that encapsulated many of the concerns of 1970s architecture, as well as the distinct edginess of a society that had to contend with everything from the Cold War to suburban sprawl. Underhill was "something of a rarity these days", wrote *Concrete Quarterly*. "It looks as if it would be a joy to live in."[27]

The owner of Underhill was an architect called Arthur Quarmby. He had designed the house for his family as "anti-architecture... a form in which everything happens secretly, within". It had been almost completely dug into the hillside—helping it to gain planning permission in an Area of Outstanding Beauty—and was contained within 8-inch-thick reinforced-concrete retaining walls. It was meant to leave as little trace on the landscape as possible, but also suggested a retreat from society. In what sounds now like a slightly paranoid touch, Quarmby even installed a periscope in the kitchen so that he could overlook the driveway.

Underhill was part of a growing movement of "geotecture", or underground architecture, and several specialist courses had recently been launched at US universities. The oil crisis had

heightened anxieties about energy use, and the idea of homes with massive insulated walls of concrete and banked earth was inherently appealing. There was also, of course, the gnawing possibility that things would soon get far worse—one of the principal roles of the geotects was to explore the possibilities of lunar and planetary habitation.

But Quarmby's house was no survivalist's bunker. Laid out like a "medieval manor house" with four wings off a central space, at its heart was a subterranean playground for the family. This was "a cave-like space with overhanging stone walls, palm trees, creepers, a grotto with a peat fire and well" beneath a "faceted, jewel-like" rooflight of acrylic and aluminium. There was a swimming pool and, on a mezzanine above it, a music room with a stage. If an indoor pool sounds a little energy-intensive for geotecture, the family soon found that its air-handling units weren't needed, and the water helped to regulate internal conditions.

Quarmby and his family lived in the house until 2016, and it is now being considered for listing. Its grass-domed, hobbit-like charm soon earned Quarmby the nickname "the Tolkien of architecture", which *Concrete Quarterly* for one saw as no insult: "Tolkien's hobbit houses had much to commend them, lacking only the principle of rooflights...."

Jarva Line
Stockholm, Sweden
Per Reimers, Michael Granit

Issue 119, Winter 1978

Above: A vast lantern lights the sprayed concrete walls and ceilings of Tekniska Hogskolan Station.

Right: Stylised foliage painted on sprayed concrete surfaces at T-Centralen Station.

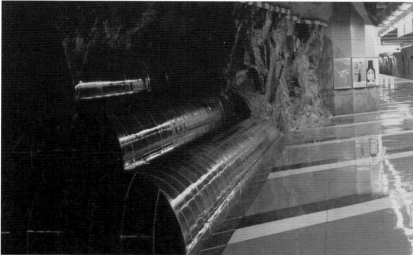

For *Concrete Quarterly*, one aspect of the modern age was, above all others, beyond redemption: the rat race. "The long-suffering commuter is not to be envied", began one editorial back in 1965, "struggling into London and back daily from the suburbs and beyond: about a million and a quarter people surge in on the morning tide, and out again in the evening."[28] By the late 1970s, things had got worse: the London Underground had become "a traumatic experience with its eerie tunnels and passages, and terrifying claustrophobia in rush hours. Were it not for expediency... nobody in their right mind would ever go into it."[29]

It was with ill-disguised envy, therefore, that the magazine introduced the 11 new stations on Stockholm Metro's Jarva line, which were already being described as the longest art gallery in the world. "Travellers may find themselves in a world of blue grottos, transported through caves of unimagined splendour and fantasy, or floating through luminous vaults of marine life and vegetation", *Concrete Quarterly* reported of this unlikely yet almost-enjoyable commuting experience.

The Jarva line stations were part of a continuous cave blasted out of rock (due to new blasting techniques, it cost about the same to build a railway in a tunnel in 1970s Stockholm as on the surface). The cave's walls were then sprayed with 70 millimetres of concrete, which the architects in charge, Per Reimers and Michael Granit, decided to treat as a 14-kilometre-long canvas.

A series of Swedish artists were invited to let their imaginations run wild, using the surfaces as a background for paintings, patterns and sculptures.

One of the stations, Kungsträdgården, looked like a kind of underground baroque garden, with vaulted concrete ceilings painted green like foliage, and copies of sculptures from the seventeenth-century palace Makalös flanking the rough cave walls. Reimers explained to *Concrete Quarterly* that the design was a reference to the park directly above:

The elms in the Kungsträdgården became well known in 1971 as demonstrations were held to preserve them... accordingly, the greenery has been recreated in the subway, unfolding like a curtain.

There were petrified concrete thickets and a copy of one of the elms on the concourse. It was as if the whole park had been plunged into a subterranean realm.

1   Wood, Alfred, "1965–75: Discovering the Environment", *Concrete Quarterly*, Issue 144, Spring 1985, p 33.

2   Calder, Barnabas, *Raw Concrete: The Beauty of Brutalism*, London: William Heinemann, 2016, p 6.

3   Jefferson, Bryan, "1975–85: The Years of Uncertainty", *Concrete Quarterly*, Issue 144, Spring 1985, p 39.

4   Perkin, George, "Editorial", *Concrete Quarterly*, Issue 93, Summer 1972, p 1.

5   Perkin, George, "Editorial", *Concrete Quarterly*, Issue 95, Winter 1972, p 1.

6   See *Concrete Quarterly*, Issue 122, Autumn 1979.

7   Perkin, George, "Editorial", *Concrete Quarterly*, Issue 100, Spring 1974, p 1.

8   Perkin, George, 'Editorial', *Concrete Quarterly*, Issue 112, Spring 1977, p 1.

9   "Precast Pavilion", *Concrete Quarterly*, Issue 86, Autumn 1970, p 2.

10   Ponti, Gio, "Taranto Cathedral", *Concrete Quarterly,* Issue 91, Winter 1971, pp 25–34. Subsequent quotations from Ponti are from this piece.

11   Campbell, Betty, "Gio Ponti", *Concrete Quarterly*, Issue 33, Summer 1957, p 34.

12   Perkin, George, "Houses at Castellaras", *Concrete Quarterly*, Issue 87, Winter 1970, pp 20–25. Subsequent quotations from Perkin are from pp 20–25 of this feature.

13   Perkin, "Houses at Castellaras", p 21.

14   Zunz, Jack, "The End of the Saga", reproduced from *The Arup Journal* in *Concrete Quarterly*, Issue 99, Winter 1973, pp 43–47. Subsequent quotations are from this feature.

15   Perkin, George, "Cathedral Craft", *Concrete Quarterly*, Issue 100, Spring 1974, p 24. Subsequent quotations are from pp 22–32 of this feature.

16   Harwood, Elain, *Space, Hope and Brutalism: English Architecture 1945–1975*, New Haven, CT: Yale University Press, 2016, p 456.

17   "Oxford First", *Concrete Quarterly*, Issue 110, Autumn 1976, p 6. Subsequent quotations are from pp 2–8 of this feature.

18   "Commodity, Firmness and Harmony", *Concrete Quarterly*, Issue 129, Summer 1981, p 9.

19   "Commodity, Firmness and Harmony", p 9.

20   Calder, *Raw Concrete: The Beauty of Brutalism*, pp 287–302.

21   Calder, *Raw Concrete: The Beauty of Brutalism*, p 311.

22   Perkin, George, "A Personal View of the National Theatre", *Concrete Quarterly*, Issue 112, Spring 1977, pp 36–37. Subsequent quotations are from pp 36–40 of this feature.

23   Calder, *Raw Concrete: The Beauty of Brutalism*, p 319.

24   Perkin, George, "A Matter of Silhouette", *Concrete Quarterly*, Issue 99, Winter 1973, p 41.

25   Harwood, *Space, Hope and Brutalism*, p 456.

26   "Islam in Regent's Park", *Concrete Quarterly,* Issue 115, Winter 1977, p 38. Subsequent quotations are from pp 34–39 of this feature.

27   "Underground House", *Concrete Quarterly*, Issue 116, Spring 1978, p 2. Subsequent quotations are from pp 2–7 of this feature.

28   Perkin, George, "Editorial", *Concrete Quarterly*, Issue 66, Autumn 1965, p 1.

29   "Stockholm's Underground World", *Concrete Quarterly*, Issue 119, Winter 1978, p 19. Subsequent quotations are from pp 19–22 of this feature.

1980–1989

Le Volcan
Le Havre, France
Oscar Niemeyer
Issue 146, Autumn 1985

Concrete Quarterly was now in colour. At least, it was some of the time. Black-and-white architectural photography could still be pleasingly atmospheric, but it rarely told the whole story.

Although we all think of concrete as grey, the more you study its colour the more you realize that there is grey and grey and grey: warm pinkish or buff greys, for instance, and cold bluish greys. These subtle variations in colour... can radically alter the character of a building. Apart from which, there is also the value of colour *against* concrete....[1]

Colour had always played an important role in concrete architecture—whether it was the blues and ochres of the Monastery of La Tourette, the brilliant greens and scarlets of the National Theatre foyers (the subject of the magazine's first colour photograph) or the rich tobacco carpet of Clifton Cathedral. The irony was that, just as printing technology was enabling *Concrete Quarterly* to show these buildings in their true colours, concrete was disappearing from sight.

The early 1980s marked a low point for concrete in Britain, and a crisis of confidence for *Concrete Quarterly* itself. The poor quality of many 1960s housing estates was clear for all to see. Reinforced concrete had been used indiscriminately, with little thought given to how durable the material might prove to be; weathering and corroded reinforcement erupted like a virus. The cheap, fast building programmes of the 1960s were "an extreme and unfortunate phase", *Concrete Quarterly* editor George Perkin concluded, adding ominously that the only concrete finishes that were now widely acceptable to the public were roofing and paving blocks.[2] He doubted the wisdom of exposing concrete externally in such a rainy climate. And if the editor of the country's leading concrete architecture magazine was saying that, the general public were likely to be putting it more strongly.

The magazine began to champion the idea of an architecture that was less in thrall to new technologies, and more of an evolutionary process, arising naturally out of heritage and tradition. "I am convinced that buildings should have a sense of place and have become, throughout the world, far too anonymous and similar", Perkin wrote on his twenty-fifth anniversary in the editor's chair.[3] This was not a defence of pastiche; it was simply a plea for a greater respect for context. Bryan Jefferson, former president of the Royal Institute of British Architects, echoed the sentiment when he looked back on the troubled decade from 1975 to 1985:

> Perhaps these recent years of uncertainty will, with hindsight, prove to be the threshold of a new period of sensitive and humane design, with technology in its rightful place—as the servant and not the master of our society.[4]

But even as attitudes towards building technology became less excitable, it was still building technology that would offer the way forward. The engineering journalist Hugh Ferguson wrote in 1988 that great strides had been made on making the material more durable. "Whole new industries have burgeoned and blossomed in the fields of concrete inspection, repair and protection", he noted, adding,

> There are now solutions to most, if not all, past problems and they are being applied by people who are today using concrete more intelligently than—if not so excitingly as—their predecessors.[5]

And as the 1980s progressed, another technology was having an ever-greater impact on architecture: computer-aided design. Architects and engineers were suddenly freed to work with new forms, many of which were only realisable in a material as strong and mouldable as concrete. Structures as diverse as New Delhi's Lotus Temple and Paris' Grande Arche seemed to declare a future in which, once again, anything was possible.

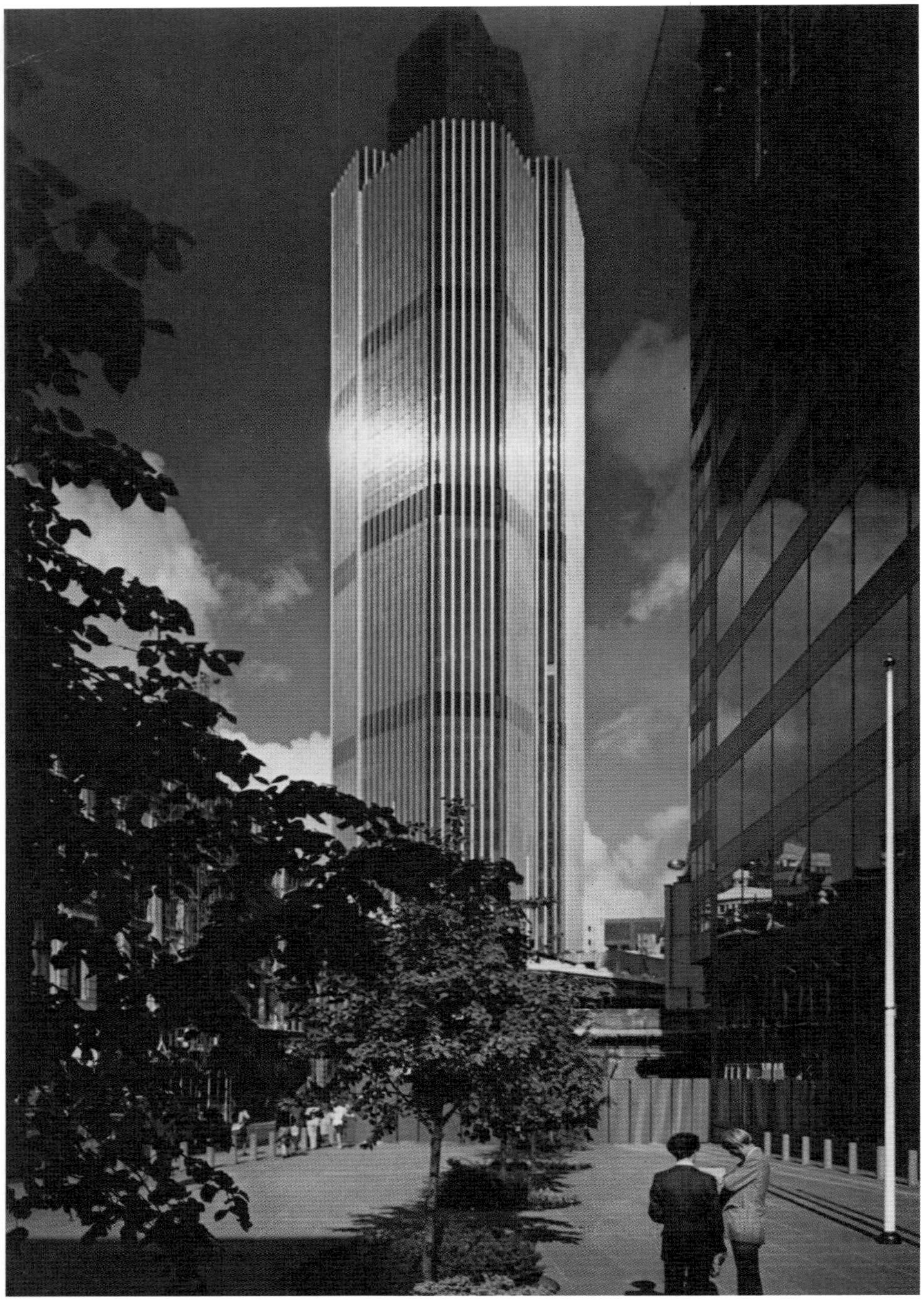

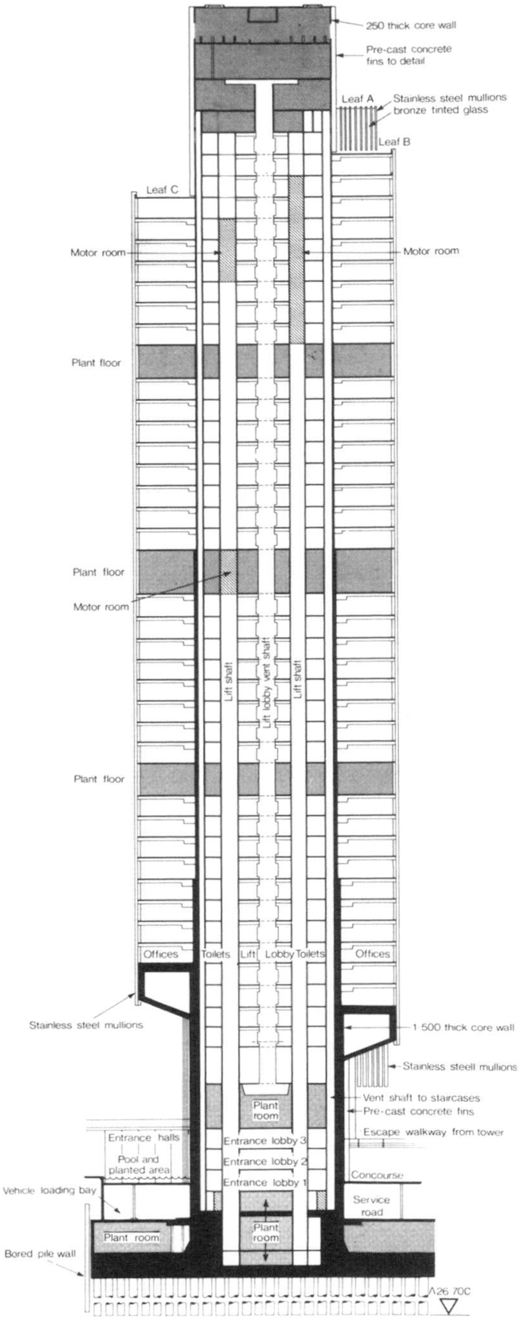
250 thick core wall
Pre-cast concrete fins to detail
Leaf A
Stainless steel mullions bronze tinted glass
Leaf B
Leaf C
Motor room
Motor room
Plant floor
Plant floor
Motor room
Lift shaft
Lift lobby vent shaft
Lift shaft
Plant floor
Offices
Toilets
Lift
Lobby
Toilets
Offices
Stainless steel mullions
1 500 thick core wall
Stainless steell mullions
Vent shaft to staircases
Pre-cast concrete fins
Plant room
Escape walkway from tower
Entrance halls
Pool and planted area
Entrance lobby 3
Entrance lobby 2
Entrance lobby 1
Concourse
Vehicle loading bay
Service road
Plant room
Plant room
Bored pile wall

NatWest Tower (Tower 42)
London, UK
Richard Seifert and Partners, Pell Frischmann

Issue 129, Summer 1981

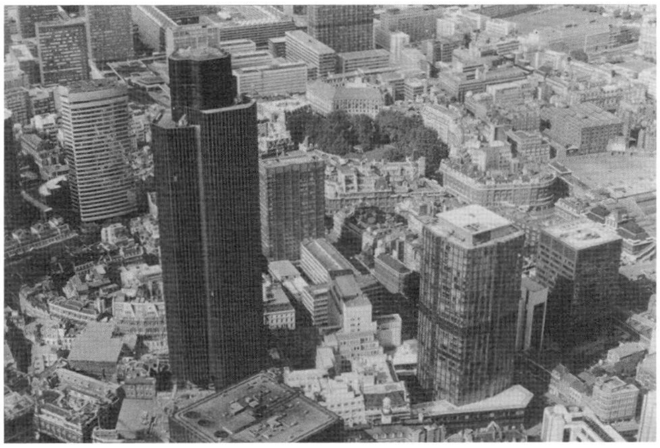

Opposite left: Stainless steel vertical
fins emphasised the height of the tower.

Opposite right: Vertical section showing
two of the 9-metre-deep cantilevers.

Opposite bottom: Aerial view showing
the 183-metre-high building towering over
the City.

Below: Typical floor plan—the ratio of core
to lettable floor space came in for criticism.

Right: The lift lobby at the heart of
the building.

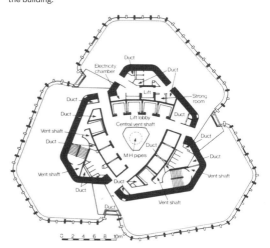

At 183 metres and 52 floors, in 1981 the NatWest Tower became the tallest building in Britain. But both its architect and *Concrete Quarterly* were in an Eeyorish mood in the face of this modern engineering triumph. The magazine observed that the office block was "an unfashionable building type" and that, in the wake of "ill-fated tower blocks of flats", all towers were now viewed with suspicion. The NatWest Tower had attracted controversy since the project's inception, partly because of its height and partly because of Richard Seifert's proposal to demolish the neighbouring Grade I-listed banking hall, dating from 1865. The hall was spared but the reception to Seifert's tower was still lukewarm. "It is a strange paradox that modern British architects appear to be subjected to much abuse at home and so much praise abroad", the architect grumbled to *Concrete Quarterly*.[6]

The exhilaration that the magazine had felt walking through 1950s Milan, where the "upward was everywhere" and the Pirelli Tower made high-rise working seem impossibly cool, seemed a distant memory.[7] Centre Point, London's answer to the Pirelli, and arguably Seifert's finest building, had only just found an occupier 13 years after its completion. The romance of high-rise commercial architecture had definitely fizzled. Where the tapering plan of both the Pirelli and Centre Point had appeared sleek and modern, the NatWest Tower's clover-leaf shape just seemed nakedly commercial. Could it be argued that, in cut-throat 1980s London, an enormous tower based on a bank's corporate logo was actually a sensitive response to context?

Each 'leaf' was a wing of office accommodation, which surrounded a massive reinforced concrete core. With walls 1.5 metres thick, the sheer bulk of this central trunk was the key not only to the structure but also to the whole look of the building. The wings did not rise from the ground but started at varying levels, and were supported on very deep, reinforced concrete cantilevers springing from the core. Each was of a different height, giving a stepped profile to the top of the tower. In an arrangement reminiscent of Frank Lloyd Wright's Johnson Wax Research Tower, the floors were like branches, projecting up to 9 metres on lightweight in-situ concrete slabs.

One effect of this structure was that the base of the tower trod relatively lightly on the dense network of City streets, its 6-metre-high plinth little wider than the central core. Nor were the facades weighed down visually by a heavy frame. Instead, they were faced with walls of bronzed glass and spandrels and stainless-steel ribs, which gave a strong vertical emphasis and increased the tower's apparent slenderness. Despite everything, the tower was a "gleaming and sophisticated presence in the City", *Concrete Quarterly* concluded.

There was a downside to this structural approach. Surprisingly for an architect as commercially savvy as Seifert, the main issue was the limit the huge core placed on lettable floor space. NatWest never moved its trading operations into the building, and moved out altogether in 1998. But the tower's distinctive form, amid the City's more anonymous mid-rise buildings, has continued to attract tenants—and arguably inspired the more recent wave of iconic commercial skyscrapers such as Norman Foster's 30 St Mary Axe and Richard Rogers' Leadenhall Building.

Concrete Quarterly was in no doubt that Seifert's contribution to high-rise architecture deserved greater recognition and should be freed from the taint of the tower block:

The towers that have come from the offices of Richard Seifert and Partners over the last two decades, will probably go down not only as the most handsome office towers that the twentieth century ever built but also as the most striking contribution of the century to London's skyline.

127

Barbican Arts Centre
London, UK
Chamberlin, Powell and Bon,
Ove Arup and Partners

Issue 134, Autumn 1982

Opposite: The auditoria were "the best to be found anywhere in the world".

Right: "Metropolitan café life" on the terrace beside the lake and fountains.

It is testament to *Concrete Quarterly's* uneasy relationship with high-rise housing in the 1970s that the three 123-metre-high concrete towers of London's Barbican Estate, completed between 1973 and 1976, were never even mentioned by the magazine. This was despite the fact that the Barbican was, in historian Barnabas Calder's words, "the ultimate Brutalist council estate"—albeit one in which the towers were not for the working class, but "for the rich workers of the City of London, peppered with such architects and creative types as [could] afford the high prices".[8]

Concrete Quarterly finally broke its silence in 1982 when editor George Perkin visited the estate's labyrinthine arts centre, which had recently opened. Its vastness—together with its slight air of impenetrability—very much shaped his initial impressions.

> Confronted by acres of orange carpet on different levels, you will be at once impaled on the horns of several dilemmas. Should you go to a play, a concert, a film, an art exhibition, the restaurant, the bar, the café, the terrace...?[9]

Perkin decided that the best course was to turn around and head back out to the terrace. "Here, there is a real suggestion of metropolitan café life. City gents—the genuine article—can be seen reading the *Financial Times* at café tables beside the fountains."

It was an opportunity for Perkin finally to assess those three mighty towers, as they cast their shadows over the *FT* readers.

> Seen from this angle, the blocks have a certain dark and brooding majesty. But are they really for people? Beside you, a small tree struggles symbolically upwards in the first years of life. Is it not, you wonder, like hanging a daisy chain around the tiger's neck?

Back inside, Perkin noted the sombre planes of bush-hammered concrete—an extension of the technique used throughout the estate and "carried out with single-minded devotion to the cause of consistency". Out of context, he thought, the roughened surfaces might have suggested armouries rather than arts, but he liked the way they were carefully balanced with other materials. With the foil of luxury finishes and the softening effect of carpets, they became "more human, though seeming to remind us that the arts are, after all, a serious business".

When he had visited London's other concrete bastion of the arts, the National Theatre, five years earlier, Perkin had reserved his greatest praise for the foyers, noting how auditoria are often glimpsed obliquely, and all the attention is on the stage.[10] But at the Barbican, the concert hall and theatre were spectacles in their own right:

> These are fine auditoria, the best to be found anywhere in the world and the crowning glories of the arts centre. Spacious, serene, comfortable, well ventilated, acoustically excellent with perfect vision—what else could we ask of an auditorium?

As with the halls and foyers, the balance of concrete with warm wood and rich dark upholstery was deftly handled. And in the theatre, there was the bonus of "your own individual door to your own individual gangway, lending a sense of occasion to the business of finding your seat".

Leaving was another matter, with Perkin noting that the underground station was closed after 10pm on Saturday and all day on Sundays.

> But then Londoners are used to battling their way to the arts—struggling along windswept walkways on the South Bank, and now negotiating the whims of London Transport to reach the nether regions of the City. It all goes to prove, as the Barbican Centre certainly does, that the spirit of human endeavour and enterprise in the face of great obstacles hasn't deserted us yet. Those who got it all going deserve medals.

THE WORLD RECAST: 70 BUILDINGS FROM 70 YEARS OF *CONCRETE QUARTERLY*

Opposite: Semi-circular staircase tower overlooking the cafe terrace, lake and City buildings in the distance.

Right: Entrance doors to each gangway in the theatre "lend a sense of occasion to the business of finding your seat".

Ismaili Centre
London, UK
Casson Conder Partnership

Issue 139, Winter 1983

Above: Exterior showing the Social Hall
windows in teak, polished steel and
bevelled glass.

Right: Entrance to the public exhibition
gallery viewed from across Cromwell
Road.

Left: Detail showing the specially treated pale grey granite, with blue inserts and edgings, fixed to the in-situ concrete walls.

Below: The entrance hall, typical of the cool, near-white interiors.

The Ismaili Centre was as close as 1980s South Kensington was prepared to get to an exposed concrete structure. It was clad in polished granite but, as *Concrete Quarterly* was quick to point out, it was *extremely thin* granite, and flashed more than a suggestion of the sculpted concrete mass beneath.

> [It is] detailed so that it always appears as a skin and nothing more, thereby lending a sharp clarity to the general profile.... In the upper part of the building, the frank expression of this thinness, together with the louvred slots for services, gives a card-like quality.[11]

As this covert modernism suggests, the Ismaili Centre is an enigmatic building: a slightly brooding if lavishly detailed five-storey block that steps back as it rises and is largely concealed behind thin vertical windows. *Concrete Quarterly* put this elusiveness down to its unique cultural and geographical context. The centre was commissioned by the Aga Khan, the leader of the Ismaili Muslims, as a religious and cultural centre for the UK's growing Ismaili community. But unlike Frederick Gibberd's Central Mosque in Regent's Park, this was never intended to be a work of explicitly Islamic architecture. The Aga Khan, who worked closely with Neville Conder and Hugh Casson at each stage of the design, stipulated that the Centre should be "essentially a London building, not necessarily derived from Islamic precedents but in keeping with their mood". Conder confirmed:

> There has been no direct reference to the Islamic architecture of other countries, no use of copy books for form or pattern, although it will be obvious to all that there have been influences at work which did not have their origins in Greece or Rome.

The idea of a 'London building' proved as vague as it always had been. The site, amid South Kensington's grand museums and stuccoed Victorian villas, was prestigious, described by one writer at the time as the most prominent plot of development land in west London. Conder proposed a simple but strongly modelled form that would "respond to the surrounding diversity" without necessarily "toning in". The building's distinctive chamfered setbacks, formed from in-situ concrete, were dictated by the daylight requirements of the houses opposite, while its generally low profile allowed clear views of the spires and domes of the museums and the Brompton Observatory.

While the hunkered, reinforced concrete form was urban and modern, there were many subtle allusions to an Islamic 'mood', as *Concrete Quarterly* put it. The 'card-like' cladding, which sparkled with blue granite, lightened the effect of the mass and "was evocative of the flat, thin facings often to be found in Islamic architecture". The use of very small, narrow panes of bevelled glass in teak window frames and doors was another "particularly pleasing detail"—the bevelling taking up so much of the glass that the panes became semi-opaque, elevating privacy over the Western notion of transparency.

Conder noted that certain "key qualities" had been given precedence, including lightness of colour, reflective and sparkling finishes, and flat planes with only the subtlest modulations of surface. "These factors, disciplined by geometry, were deemed to be conducive to a sense of serenity." The result was a building that *Concrete Quarterly* found to be "unassertive, eloquent and beautifully detailed... an extremely skilful fusion of East and West".

Le Volcan
Le Havre, France
Oscar Niemeyer

Issue 146, Autumn 1985

The two main elements of the Cultural Centre—the theatre on the left and the lower multi-purpose hall on the right.

A sculptural ramp of reinforced concrete snakes its way up from the basement to the ground floor.

The UK may not have been the most hospitable climate for flamboyant concrete architecture in the 1980s, but just across the English Channel, the wind was still blowing in a favourable direction. "Oscar Niemeyer's Cultural Centre in Le Havre seems like a bit of old times", wrote *Concrete Quarterly* of the 77-year-old's latest work—a theatre and concert hall in two sweeping skirts of board-marked concrete.

> Here are the authentic marks of the Brazilian master: bold and curvaceous geometric forms of dramatic simplicity exploiting the sculptural possibilities of reinforced concrete—Brasília come to Europe—proclaiming in every sweeping line that Modern Architecture Rules OK.[12]

Both buildings were in exposed concrete. The lower concert hall was a regular circle in plan, curving inwards as it rose, with lozenge-shaped windows piercing its wall. The larger volcano-like structure was asymmetrical, flaring out on one side to follow the sectional arrangement of the theatre and cinema housed within. They were connected by a vast square plinth, containing a foyer, shops and public spaces, while a sculptural ramp of reinforced concrete snaked its way up from the basement-level square to the ground floor.

It was all "very Niemeyer", and recalled Gio Ponti's remark that some buildings were only possible to imagine in concrete. "It is surely true to say that reinforced concrete was the only material that could have been used to achieve these curved volumes", wrote *Concrete Quarterly,* "although the reverse is also true: the volumes are the result of the structural possibilities of the material." It was the type of iconic building that was almost extinct in 1980s Britain, one where structural virtuosity sometimes seemed to be the whole point:

> The building succeeds, surely, simply because it is a monument in its own right, making no attempt… to be part of the town fabric or to blend harmoniously with it.

Concrete Quarterly wondered about the wisdom of so much exposed concrete in a climate so similar to Britain's, and noted that the concrete surfaces of Niemeyer's Brasília buildings were invariably and immaculately clad in white marble. But Le Havre was a city that knew its concrete—after it was severely bombed during the Second World War, it was largely rebuilt by the pioneer of reinforced concrete architecture, Auguste Perret. The city's administration was comfortable with the material, it wanted Niemeyer, "and all obstacles disappeared at the sound of such a famous name".

Concrete Quarterly pondered whether a British council would have been quite so star-struck (if indeed it had been in a position to undertake such a grand cultural project in the first place). "Questions, of course, immediately arise about this building in the prosaic British mind. Would it get past the planning committee in Worthing, or indeed Westminster?" To admirers of modern architecture, the English Channel had probably never seemed wider.

Queen Elizabeth II Conference Centre
London, UK
Powell & Moya

Issue 150, Autumn 1986

Above: The structure is emphasised
with textured white concrete elements.

Right: The centre occupies a "daunting
position" directly opposite Westminster
Abbey.

Two views of the Benjamin Britten Lounge overlooking Westminster Abbey. All the beam and wall surfaces are of textured white concrete.

If expressed concrete structures weren't exactly the flavour of the decade, nobody had told Philip Powell and Hidalgo Moya. The pair had, perhaps more than any other practice, defined the look of Britain's post-war university and hospital buildings, and that look more often than not involved textured, structural concrete. Now, 40 years after their first commission, and still "unwaveringly consistent in their devotion to expressing the structure of a building, both inside and out",[13] they had been handed one of the most daunting, historically sensitive sites in Europe:

> looking straight into the north face of Westminster Abbey, rubbing shoulders with the Central Hall on the one hand and the Middlesex Guildhall on the other, and just round the corner from the Palace of Westminster and Big Ben.

The building in question was the Queen Elizabeth II Conference Centre, and there was never any question of it just quietly fitting in. The surroundings may have been historic but the functional requirements were all about the demands of 1980s business and the booming conference market. In particular, the large auditoriums needed unobstructed floor spaces and acoustic separation, and the overall plan required a high degree of adaptability. In response, Powell & Moya expressed their wish to "produce a building expressive of our times... a structure of flexibility and strength with well-defined visual qualities". They considered that only in-situ reinforced concrete, carefully specified and finished, could satisfy all these needs.

The concrete was exposed throughout the interior and on the external structural elements, with all the surfaces textured using a medium-point tool. The mix chosen included white cement, Cornish silver-grey Luxulyan granite and Cornish sand, leaving "a slight sparkle in the aggregate". It was the kind of finish made for *Concrete Quarterly*'s new era of colour photography, with the crisp whiteness of the concrete "thrown up with artificial lighting, and everywhere enhanced by direct juxtaposition with soft carpets, coloured fabrics and the pale beech furniture". Particularly impressive was the diagrid of concrete beams across the conference halls, which allowed for uninterrupted spans of 34 metres and was picked out with inset coloured lighting.

Concrete Quarterly was less sure about the external finish—the magazine had been warning against the use of white concrete in Britain's wet climate for years. While it approved of the strong emphasis these structural elements gave to horizontal and vertical lines, it worried about whether they would "keep their present crispness as time goes on". But perhaps that was for another day. For the moment, it was just glad to see masters at work, doing what they did best:

> At a time when concrete is not exactly going through its most popular phase, it is courageous that the architects should have stuck with it and made it, in fact, one of the most attractive architectural features of this building.

The grillage of white concrete beams
and columns in the main auditorium.

The main conference room. Artificial
lighting was used throughout to
highlight the texture and sparkling
aggregate of the concrete structure.

1980–1989

Lotus Temple
New Delhi, India
Fariburz Sahba,
Flint & Neill

Issue 152, Spring 1987

Above: The concrete shells of the petals are covered externally with white marble from Greece.

Right: Internally, the double-layered dome is made up of 54 reinforced concrete ribs with shells between.

Below: The dome is supported on arches the shape of parabolic conoids.

Right: Detail of the concrete-ribbed ceiling. The concrete has a bush-hammered finish.

Computers changed the course of concrete architecture. By the late 1980s, the material's strength and plasticity—the characteristics that had so appealed to structural engineers—could suddenly be modelled more quickly and accurately, unleashing an array of increasingly complex, sculptural shapes. In the 1950s, when Félix Candela and Pier Luigi Nervi had raised structural engineering to an art form, they had claimed the primacy of their own intuition over mathematics. Now, digital technology was bringing construction back to cold, hard, immutable numbers.

The UK wasn't yet in the mood for displays of virtuosic structural design, but on the plains outside New Delhi, a building had unfolded that showed the astonishing possibilities of computer-aided design. The Lotus Temple looked like the Sydney Opera House reassembled as a vast white flower, with three layers of nine marble-clad petals. The inner two curved inwards, while the outer one curled away to provide sheltered entrance canopies.

The temple was a house of worship for the Bahá'í faith, but Iranian-born architect Fariburz Sahba chose the lotus form for its symbolism throughout India's religions. This reflected Bahá'í's stress on the "oneness of mankind"—a selling point that Concrete Quarterly found "immensely appealing".[14] Bahá'í's all-embracing approach extended to architecture, the only stipulations for its temples being that they must be nine-sided and must have natural daylight. Sahba was therefore free to continue the lotus concept to the internal dome, which was shaped like the inside of a bud, reaching up to a glazed tip.

Unlike most organic forms, the symmetrical lotus was inherently buildable, but the shapes involved were supremely complex. Using computer-generated diagrams, it was decided that the outer petals would have spherical surfaces while the inner petals would be toroidal. The dome was made up of 54 reinforced concrete ribs with shells between, supported on arches the shape of parabolic conoids—the age of the computer had also ushered in a whole new vocabulary of geometry. "Ten years ago it would have been impossible to realise the design so faithfully and elegantly", wrote Concrete Quarterly. "A far more simplistic approach would have been required, with at least two years longer for completion."

The shells for the petals were made from unusually thin reinforced concrete—200 millimetres for the inner leaves and just 135 millimetres for the canopies. This called for advanced stress analysis, again using computer models. When it came to their construction, however, there was no substitute for manpower. The forms for the petals were built in their entirety from plywood and timber at ground level before being hoisted into position by crane. The inner petals were poured three at a time, in two lifts, while the outer canopies were realised in a continuous pour. Much of the concrete was placed by workers carrying back-breaking 50-pound loads—a reminder that while the digital age may have brought new structural possibilities, in much of the world construction was, and still is, a labour-intensive struggle.

Royal Hospital
Muscat, Oman
Percy Thomas Partnership

Issue 156, Spring 1988

Above left: Domes were of in-situ
concrete cast with permanent
GRP liners.

Above right: Internal court showing
the relief pattern achieved by spandrel
panels cast against GRP moulds.

Right: The hospital appears as a
gleaming white building in the scrub
and desert landscape.

Below: Pierced concrete blocks provide a strong decorative element for internal corridors.

Right: The pointed arch panels were precast and were introduced after a government edict for a more indigenous type of architecture.

Below right: Waiting area in the VIP suite.

With the profession at a low ebb in Britain, architects began to look abroad. Throughout the late 1970s and 1980s, British practices took on a number of commissions in the Middle East, where they were held in particularly high esteem.[15] Among this early wave of globe-trotting firms was the Percy Thomas Partnership, architect of Clifton Cathedral, which in 1982 was appointed to prepare a 'Health Plan' for the government of Oman. Six years later, its consortium with British contractor George Wimpey had completed the Royal Hospital, a £147 million, 629-bed facility in the desert outside Muscat. Back in Britain, *Concrete Quarterly* "cast an envious glance at what is, no doubt, one of the most lavish and well-equipped hospitals in the world".[16] The NHS this wasn't— among the provisions was a self-contained VIP suite with 12 private bedrooms and a separate entrance.

It was, however, a fine example of the architectural use of concrete—both in situ and precast. "With its cool and airy vaulted spaces, cream painted concrete and marble reception areas, it suitably combines Islamic splendour with the practical requirements of modern medicine", noted *Concrete Quarterly*. Omani heritage was reflected in the repetitive use of arches, colonnades, domes and barrel vaults. The frame was built from in-situ reinforced concrete, with vaults cast using timber formwork and domes with permanent glass-reinforced plastic (GRP) liners.

Traditional decorative motifs were re-interpreted using modern techniques. Delicate grilles were formed from precast concrete, while facade panels were cast against GRP moulds to create a strong relief pattern, 10 millimetres deep. But there was clearly some concern that the design was too western. Midway through construction, with the building already at first-floor level, the government issued an edict that all new buildings should be more indigenous in design. This led Percy Thomas to introduce the precast pointed-arch panels that are one of the most prominent features of the facade.

Site conditions posed a number of problems throughout the 43-month project. No road existed and essential services such as electricity and water had to be laid specially over a great distance. The British-led consortium needed to house and feed a workforce of up to 2,500 people, and work was undertaken in temperatures reaching 46 degrees Celsius. *Concrete Quarterly* saw the quality of the final building, and its completion in record time, as a cause for "British pride—not all that commonly aired these days".

La Grande Arche de la Défense
Paris, France
Johan Otto von Spreckelsen,
Aéroports de Paris

Issue 161, Summer 1989

Above: The upper bridge was cast in situ 110 metres above ground.

Right: La Grande Arche is essentially a hollow concrete cube 110 metres along each side, with a central void measuring 70 metres in each direction.

THE WORLD RECAST: 70 BUILDINGS FROM 70 YEARS OF *CONCRETE QUARTERLY*

The primary elements are four vertical prestressed concrete 'frames' linked by structural floors at seven-storey intervals.

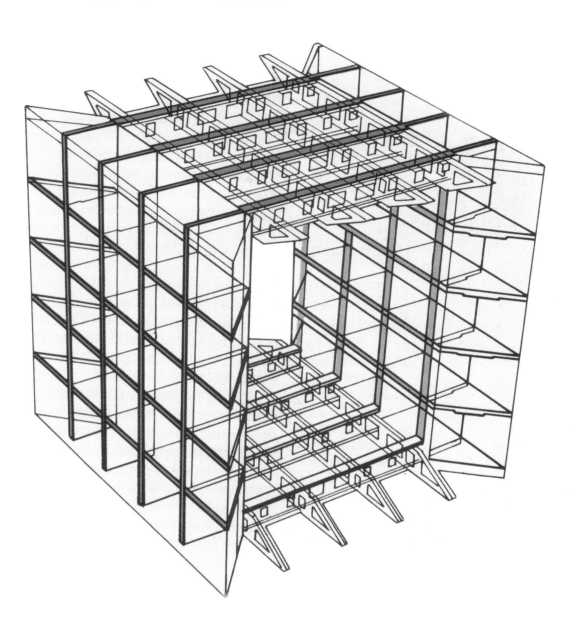

La Grande Arche de la Défense was "both arch and cube, and yet it is neither", wrote *Concrete Quarterly* in 1989.[17] If that makes it sound in some way ambiguous, it was not. La Grande Arche was an enormous monument, in a city famed for its enormous monuments. The Eiffel Tower had been built to celebrate the centenary of the French Revolution; la Grande Arche would celebrate the bicentenary. It was, from its very inception, intended to be one of the iconic buildings of the twentieth century.

But *Concrete Quarterly*'s gnomic description was entirely accurate. This was both a simple structure and an extraordinary one—which would require all the construction nous of one of Europe's biggest building firms, Bouygues, to make a reality. La Grande Arche was essentially a vast hollow cube, 110 metres along each side, with a central void measuring 70 metres in each direction—"large enough to completely swallow the cathedral of Notre Dame, spire and all". Each vertical side was a 35-storey office tower, connected by bridges spanning the void at the top and bottom. It looked like "a space-age version of Stonehenge, assembled by some gigantic latter-day Druid using office blocks instead of bluestone megaliths", wrote *Concrete Quarterly*. The comparison was more appropriate than you might think. The arch was in fact a vast monolith, containing not

a single expansion joint, and resting on, but not attached to, its foundations. "It could quite literally be picked up, turned over, and put down again."

Not that anyone was likely to try. The mighty concrete frame weighed upwards of 300,000 tonnes, much of which was accounted for by its primary structural elements, four vast square frames known as "*les megas*". Each of these was a complete ring of prestressed concrete, running vertically through the building: "Imagine four picture frames, standing parallel to one another, and scale up by a factor of a couple of hundred or so", as *Concrete Quarterly* put it. The vertical members alone consisted of solid walls 18 metres wide, 110 metres high and 1.7 metres thick.

It was a huge amount of concrete to deposit on possibly the most contentious, fought-over development plot in Paris. At the head of the city's prime axis from the Louvre, along the Champs-Élysées, and through the Arc de Triomphe, it was also the gateway to La Défense, the commercial district that had divided opinion since the 1950s. One early office tower, which had the misfortune to rise behind the Arc de Triomphe, was described by the influential magazine *l'Architecture d'Aujourd'hui* as the "disfiguration of the very horizon where for the patriotic soul the bloody sun of Austerlitz still sets".

Despite the dangers of further inciting Parisian wrath, in 1982 President François Mitterrand launched an international design competition for the site, clearly with the bicentennial celebrations in mind. Out of 424 entrants, the winner was declared as the little-known Danish architect Johan Otto von Spreckelsen. His Grande Arche was, Mitterrand announced, "remarkable for its purity, the force with which it adds a new landmark to the historic alignment of Paris, and for its spaciousness". The countdown to Bastille Day 1989 had begun.

Such was the simplicity of the structure that some critics assumed it to be the work of a novice architect. But that did not mean it was easy to build. Bouygues had to begin by threading 12 mighty piles, each 30 metres high and 30,000 tonnes in weight, through variable subsoil and around a motorway and three rail tunnels. On top of this substructure rested the lower of the two 70-metre-span bridges and the 110-metre-high vertical walls. The amount of steel required to make the 'megas' structurally viable was immense: "To describe them as 'heavily reinforced' would be as much an understatement as calling the Grande Arche 'big'." The concrete contained up to 350 kilograms of steel per cubic metre—more than four times as much as a conventional office block. The structure also needed a 50 Newton concrete mix, nearly twice the usual strength, and high-pressure pumps to ensure that it flowed smoothly around the dense reinforcement.

But the real show of constructional ingenuity came with the fourth side of the frame—the upper bridge. Bouygues had been advised to precast this element but reasoned that, with a fixed deadline bearing down, casting in situ would be quicker as it would cause less disturbance to other site operations.

On the downside, it meant working 110 metres above ground. The company designed a 260-tonne steel falsework to support the formwork, and this in turn was supported by two 400-tonne tower cranes, which had to be taken down and reassembled for each of the four *megas*. Even so, progress was swift: although every beam swallowed over 1,000 cubic metres of concrete and had to be cast in seven sections, they each took less than a month to construct.

Concrete Quarterly could find only one very small area, "perhaps half a square metre", of poorly compacted concrete, in a non-structural floor on the upper deck—although this was possibly enough to ruin the view from the Arc de Triomphe. Otherwise the quality of the finished concrete was itself a triumph: "The *megas* have a consistently superb finish, worthy of concrete placed for architectural rather than structural reasons."

Opposite: The Arche occupies a key site on the city's prime axis from the Louvre, along the Champs-Élysées and through the Arc de Triomphe.

Right and below: The concrete frame has been left exposed in the public rooftop observatory.

1980–1989

1   Perkin, George, "Concrete in Colour", *Concrete Quarterly*, Issue 116, Spring 1978, p 19.

2   Perkin, George, "All Part of the Scene", *Concrete Quarterly*, Issue 126, Autumn 1980, p 1.

3   Perkin George, "Looking Back 25 Years", *Concrete Quarterly*, Issue 137, Summer 1983, p 15.

4   Jefferson, Bryan, "1975–1985 The Years of Uncertainty", *Concrete Quarterly*, Issue 144, Spring 1985, p 45.

5   Ferguson, Hugh, "Personal View", *Concrete Quarterly*, Issue 159, Winter 1988, p 18.

6   "Tallest Tower", *Concrete Quarterly*, Issue 129, Summer 1981, pp 14–19. All subsequent quotations in this section are from this piece unless otherwise stated.

7   "Italy", *Concrete Quarterly*, Issue 25, Summer 1955, p 10.

8   Calder, Barnabas, *Raw Concrete: The Beauty of Brutalism*, London: William Heinemann, 2016, p 87.

9   Perkin, George, "Evening at the Barbican", *Concrete Quarterly*, Issue 134, Autumn 1982, pp 22–26. All subsequent quotations in this section are from this piece unless otherwise stated.

10 Perkin, George, "Lights up: A Personal View of the National Theatre", *Concrete Quarterly*, Issue 112, 1977, pp 37–38.

11 "East Meets West in Kensington", *Concrete Quarterly*, Issue 139, Winter 1983, pp 2–7. All subsequent quotations in this section are from this piece.

12 "Niemeyer at Le Havre", *Concrete Quarterly*, Issue 146, Autumn 1985, pp 36–39. All subsequent quotations in this section are from this piece.

13 "Conference Centre", *Concrete Quarterly*, Issue 150, Autumn 1986, pp 22–27. All subsequent quotations in this section are from this piece.

14 "Lotus Petals", *Concrete Quarterly*, Issue 152, Spring 1987, pp 14–19. All subsequent quotations in this section are from this piece.

15 Perkin, George, "Quiet Confidence", *Concrete Quarterly*, Issue 107, Winter 1975, p 1.

16 "A Royal Hospital", *Concrete Quarterly*, Issue 156, Spring 1987, pp 18–21. All subsequent quotations in this section are from this piece.

17 Swan, Russ, "Tour de Force", *Concrete Quarterly*, Issue 161, Summer 1989, pp 10–17. All subsequent quotations in this section are from this piece.

1990–1999

American Air Museum
Duxford, UK
Norman Foster and Partners,
Ove Arup and Partners
Issue 177, Winter 1995

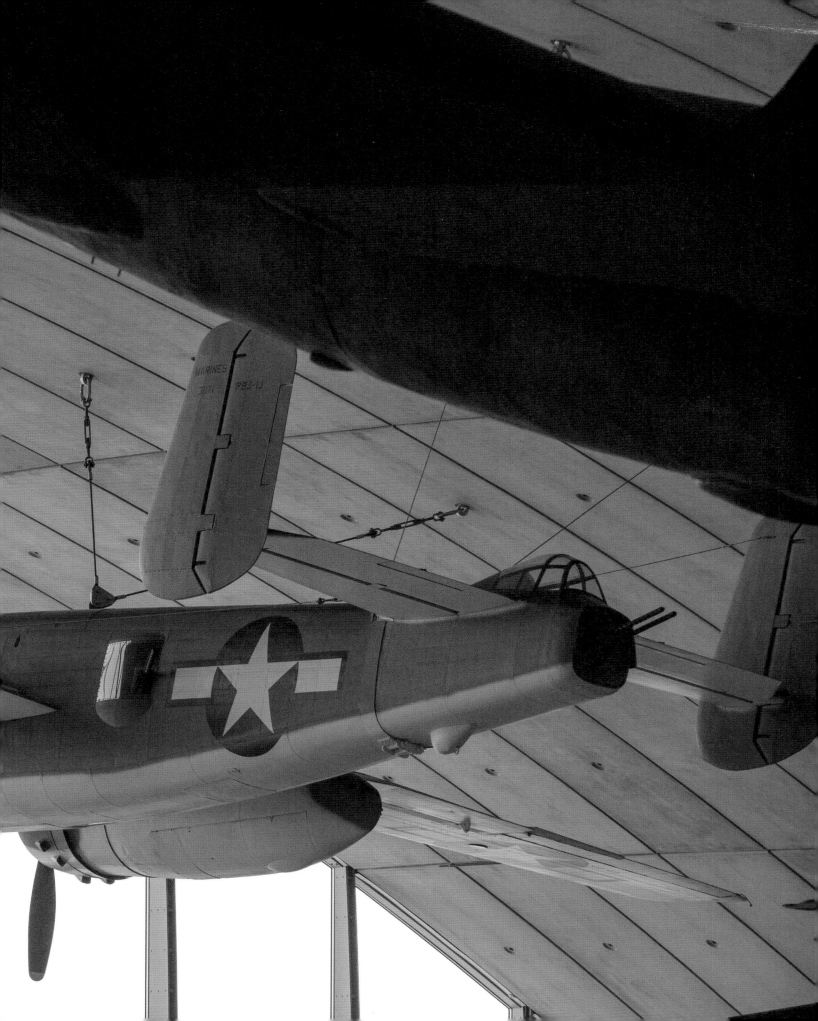

At some point in the 1990s, the tentative concrete revival became a full-blown renaissance. Architects such as Michael Hopkins and Nicholas Grimshaw, who had made their names with High Tech buildings of steel, glass and lightweight materials, were suddenly producing immaculate fair-faced concrete interiors. In London, the new stations of the Jubilee Line were bringing a stylised industrial look to transport. And at the American Air Museum in Duxford, Norman Foster was flying planes under a pristine concrete sky.

This was partly a reaction to the excesses of commercial architecture in the 1980s, when developers had bred a philosophy of putting up a structural frame as quickly as possible and then concealing it behind a succession of cosmetic layers. As John Pringle, a partner at Michael Hopkins Architects, put it in *Concrete Quarterly*:

> We often wonder why the industry chose to import only the most philistine element of American construction technology. What had happened to the superb workmanship found in the buildings of Louis Kahn, IM Pei and Paul Rudolph, where we really did have something to learn from the Americans? It seemed as though no one had asked for architectural concrete in this country since the days of the brutalist buildings of the 1960s or the National Theatre in the 1970s.[1]

Increasingly British architects turned to different architectural cultures for inspiration. In Switzerland, they discovered Peter Zumthor and Herzog & de Meuron; in Japan they found Tadao Ando. What these architects had in common was an approach that celebrated concrete's solidity and depth, but most of all its beauty as a surface material. Ando was portrayed as part mystic, part master craftsman, creating spaces of almost sacred majesty from concrete much as traditional Japanese builders had used wood, and decorating it with nothing but the ephemeral qualities of light.

Not that all ornament had been banished. In another corner of the architectural world, designers were taking an almost diametrically opposite approach to the material, revelling in its artificiality—in effect, its ability to be anything they wanted it to be. In France, Ricardo Bofill was building overblown classical palaces on housing estates, replicating ornate stone details in precast concrete. In Britain, John Outram was shaping, colouring, lacquering and patterning concrete in ever more elaborate ways, on buildings such as the Judge Institute of Management Studies in Cambridge. "Concrete has no intrinsic physical features", Outram argued. "However, rather than avoiding the issue of its blankness, we can instead use this blankness as a canvas. Concrete is a perfect medium to convey ideas."[2]

Concrete may have been enjoying a renaissance, but in some senses it was where it had always been: to some designers as natural as stone; to others as pliable as plastic. It was sacred, it was superficial, and it was everything in-between.

Antigone
Montpellier, France
Ricardo Bofill

Issue 165, Summer 1990

Above: Six vast piazzas are linked via a
1-kilometre central axis.

Right: The development stretches over
36 hectares.

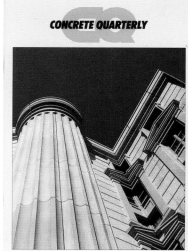

CONCRETE QUARTERLY

SUMMER 1990

Left: Cover of *Concrete Quarterly* showing a detail of the Place du Nombre d'Or, Antigone.

Below left: The Conseil Régional, built in the form of an arch.

Below right: Projecting cornices shield the apartments from the hot Mediterranean sun.

In the 1960s Oscar Niemeyer and Gio Ponti had found that concrete allowed them to imagine completely new forms. A generation later, the Catalan architect Ricardo Bofill used it to reimagine very old ones.

Bofill had established his practice, the Taller de Arquitectura, in 1963, but it wasn't until the 1970s that his signature brand of heroic hyper-classical architecture really took off, with two social housing schemes in the Parisian suburbs of Marne-la-Vallée and St Quentin-en-Yvelines. Or, as Jonathan Glancey put it in *Concrete Quarterly*, "Bofill raised two colossal classical palaces set in massive imperial Roman squares, piazzas, crescents and circuses."[3]

These gargantuan housing blocks were unlike anything ever seen before and were largely the work of the Taller's resident Englishman, Peter Hodgkinson. Actual classical palaces being prohibitively expensive, Bofill and Hodgkinson developed the next best thing. "The only way to realize such heroic architecture on a low budget was to prefabricate it", wrote Glancey. "In the era of post-war democracy a modern Versailles would be precast in factories."

In a factory on the outskirts of Paris, Hodgkinson set about breaking Bofill's designs into sections so that they could be precast in concrete, complete with pediments, pilasters and detailed ornamentation. During the casting process, the panels were also dyed, which not only gave the designs another layer of richness but also helped them to withstand the Parisian rain, "overcoming the popular prejudice against concrete as a surface building material because of its tendency to stain badly in wet climates".

Bofill's designs showed great skill, but his real genius lay in convincing local authorities to commission his grandiose schemes. He was, Glancey noted, a consummate flatterer of politicians' vanity, and had managed to secure his first public

housing project when he was still in his early 20s. In 1979, he landed his biggest project yet, an entire 36-hectare city district of Montpellier. Furnished with a suitably classical name, Antigone would occupy the practice for much of the next two decades, and would be the most complete expression of Bofill's heroic approach to housing.

"Not only do the new apartment blocks look impressively Roman but, unlike Marne-la-Vallée and St Quentin-en-Yvelines, the classicism here is more than skin deep", wrote Glancey. Refinements in the casting process had enabled Hodgkinson to include classical detailing not just on the facades but also on panels inside the apartments, which were now based on classical proportions. The approach had been adapted to the Mediterranean climate, with projecting concrete cornices shielding the apartments from the sun. The landscaping too was based on classical precedents, with balustrades, lamp standards and other components all precast in concrete.

Concrete Quarterly captured Bofill at the height of the Glasnost era, a period in which he occupied a curious position between East and West. His flamboyant classicism had won commissions for the Houston School of Music and the MoMA/Jefferson Tower in Chicago, but the grandeur and scale of his work, with echoes of the mock-aristocratic style of the mass housing built under Stalin, had also led to plans for an Antigone-esque residential extension to Moscow. Bofill may not have been to everyone's taste, but his admirers were nothing if not diverse.

David Mellor Building
London, UK
Michael Hopkins Architects

Issue 174, Autumn 1992

Above: Internally, the concrete was left exposed as a unifying element between different areas of the building. Services and light fittings were cast in.

Right: The front elevation is mainly glazed, with lead-faced panels on the side walls.

The in-situ concrete columns and
slab edges were clearly expressed
in the elevation.

The David Mellor Building by Michael Hopkins Architects was commissioned by a designer, located directly opposite London's new Design Museum, in a cluster of designer warehouses. Fair-faced concrete was used throughout—quite a statement of the material's renaissance as a finish in its own right.

The building, on a narrow site next to Tower Bridge, was to be a workshop, showroom, office and apartment for the cutlery designer David Mellor. These diverse functions were to be visually united by the fair-faced concrete walls, columns and soffits. Hopkins had little experience of the material, but was weary of the superficiality of late 1980s postmodernism. Concrete, suggested project architect John Pringle, was an honest material that hid little about the nature of a building's construction:

> We wanted it to look like concrete and not like plaster or stone or something else it wasn't.... We wanted it to look like a moulded material which had been poured. We wanted to see the profiles of the mould and were anxious not to obliterate them with heavy surface treatments.[4]

But most of all they wanted it to exude quality. Mellor, Pringle wrote, was

> a perfectionist, bringing a combination of the precision of production engineering and the art of the silversmith to the construction industry: he shared our usual preoccupation with bringing out the quality of materials used in building.

Unfortunately for his architect, the concrete industry had been badly drained of expertise during the lean years. "The skills

needed for a high-quality finish were simply not there any more", wrote Pringle, "at least not without a real struggle."

> When we went around precasters' yards they couldn't produce a single sample of fair-faced plain grey concrete mixes from their samples libraries; they were all faced with revolting bits of stone, marble tiles or terrazzo, destined for large, storey-height cladding panels for city office blocks. It was as if they were almost ashamed of concrete, the mainstay of their business.

So the architects began to learn the techniques of concrete from scratch, "with the help of some patient and committed contractors", opting instead for in-situ concrete. Like their modernist forebears, they approached it as a craft material, discovering that "formwork isn't just temporary rough carpentry to be nailed together and discarded... it had to be a beautiful piece of joinery, as good to look at as the finished product". Preparations were painstaking and, in a sign of the growing influence of Japanese concrete architecture among UK practices, they sought advice from experts in Obayashi. Every square millimetre of the forms was meticulously cleaned with compressed air immediately before concrete was delivered to site, and every particle of rust removed from the reinforcement to avoid staining.

When it came to perfecting the surface texture, Pringle went to the very top. "Tadao Ando told me that his secret was that he got all the young architects out of his office and gave them all a sheet of sandpaper to sand down the entire surface by hand", he revealed. This proved too much for Hopkins Architects, but not for Mellor. The perfectionist client picked up his sandpaper and did just that....

Waterloo International Station
London, UK
Nicholas Grimshaw,
Anthony Hunt Associates

Issue 176, Spring 1993

Opposite: The coffered platform soffits were a defining element of the departure lounge.

Right: Fair-faced concrete provided "a perfect foil to the lithe translucence of the roof above".

Railway stations rarely featured in the early years of *Concrete Quarterly*. The post-war years were the age of the car, which the magazine described with almost utopian zeal, even declaring investment in motorways as vital to a united Europe.[5] Concrete ran through the architecture of driving—not just the roads themselves, but car parks, motorway bridges and service stations. When it came to the railways, on the other hand, the age of heroic modernism coincided with an era of declining passenger numbers and chronic underinvestment. Concrete had missed the train.

Then Waterloo International came along, admittedly more of an airport terminal on rails. This was to be the end of the line for the railway through the £9 billion Channel Tunnel, one of the century's most ambitious engineering projects. It was also the first new station in central London for nearly a century. An architectural showpiece was required, and it seemed destined to be built not in concrete but in steel. This was the late 1980s, the high point of High Tech, a movement that revelled in lightweight articulated steel structures, and these seemed like the natural heirs of the great Victorian train sheds— celebrations of light, space and engineering.

From the outside, this is exactly what architect Nicholas Grimshaw delivered at Waterloo International. The building was defined by a magnificent asymmetrical steel and glass roof that snaked and tapered for half a kilometre through the packed streets west of the existing station. But that was only part of the story. The five tracks of the international terminus were essentially the top deck of a railway viaduct. Beneath them was a huge concrete-framed structure, supported off a 1.8-metre-deep reinforced raft slab, which housed the arrivals and departure lounges. This was Britain's new front door, and it was framed in exposed concrete.

Writing in *Concrete Quarterly*, project architect Steve McGuckin said that the original intention was to build the frame in steel, but analysis indicated that in-situ concrete would be 8 per cent quicker.[6] With a mere 23 months on site before the first trains rolled down the tracks, this proved a compelling case. Concrete could provide a vibration-free environment with minimal deflections under the live loads of the Eurostar's 16-carriage trains.

It could also strike a cool, understated look, ideal for sophisticated modern tourist and business travel alike. Grimshaw's decision to leave much of the concrete 'as struck' acted as "a perfect foil to the lithe translucence of the roof above", wrote McGuckin, adding that the architects favoured "the natural qualities of cast concrete, with only natural colour variation and a true reflection of the mould, to the inevitable plastered effect of large areas of 'made good' concrete". High Tech, it seemed, had gone back to nature.

This preference placed extreme pressure on the concrete pour, as there was virtually no time for extensive preparation before casting, or for demolition of areas with poor finishes: "They had to be right first time." And they were. The concrete shear walls were cast in just two pours and left no blowholes, while the coffered departure lounge soffits became something of a centrepiece, illuminated from below by uplighters. As McGuckin pointed out, any mistakes would be quickly spotted: nobody looks at a ceiling more closely than someone waiting for a train.

Tamana City Observatory
Tamana, Japan
Masaharu Takasaki

Issue 176, Spring 1993

Opposite: The 18.5-metre-high
observatory was a collage of abstract
forms.

Below: Each element was symbolic—the
three parallel shafts, pointing towards
the sky, represented the city's future.

Right: All of the concrete was cast
in situ.

Japan's late 1980s economic boom gave birth to some of the most wildly idiosyncratic architecture of modern times. A frenzy of property speculation saw architects including Hiroshi Hara, Kengo Kuma and Shin Takamatsu unleash a series of fantastically overloaded alien forms on the urban landscape. Kuma's M2 Building in Tokyo—a car showroom that followed the trajectory of the Japanese economy to become a funeral parlour—is towered over by an absurdly out-of-scale ionic column, while Hara's Umeda Sky Building even incorporated a docking platform for spaceships. Such works were products of an "unreproducible moment in time", according to the designer Adam Nathaniel Furman, "in a culture that was primed for not just allowing, but actively catalysing the most unlikely forms of architectural brilliance".[7]

One of the most unlikely forms of all came from the mind of Masaharu Takasaki. The most remarkable thing about Takasaki's 1992 Tamana City Observatory on the southern island of Kyushu was that it was actually designed to blend in with its surroundings. The 18.5-metre-high collage of abstract concrete forms was commissioned in response to growing anxieties about the pace of urbanisation. On a hill overlooking the city, this was to be a place where people could escape the grind and relax in nature. The freeform shapes, with barely a right angle among them, were intended to reflect the "organic relationship and dialogue between mankind and nature", Takasaki explained.

> The philosophy of the design has been to create a 'living body within its environment' which not only contains natural energy, but also stimulates its natural surroundings.[8]

The largest element was a large concrete egg set in a not-quite rectangular frame, around which hovered five rings. Viewing decks, perched on wonky-looking columns, thrust out apparently at random, while three perfectly parallel shafts pointed towards the sky. Every element was a symbol: the three main levels were named "earth place", "cloud place" and "star place"; the rings were lotus flowers representing the "growing peace of Tamana", and the three shafts signified the city's future. More cryptically, Takasaki named the egg-shaped element "zero cosmology".

The whole structure was cast in situ, which demanded a creative approach to preparing formwork and reinforcement, Takasaki noted.

> Many of the challenges were overcome by preparatory work at 1:50 scale, but trial and error were also involved, for instance in fixing the five subtly different lotus flowers, and the spiral staircase which was supported only at top and bottom.

For the ovoid element, a full-scale mock-up was the only way to work out how to reproduce its freehand-drawn curves; the resulting mould involved more than 320 separate plywood panels.

The observatory was a highly original take on the age-old idea of building in harmony with nature. "It is a place in which to be aware of oneself", wrote Takasaki, "to watch the day-by-day development of the community, and to ponder on the flow of time."

American Air Museum
Duxford, UK
Norman Foster and Partners,
Ove Arup and Partners

Issue 177, Winter 1995

Above: The glass wall that forms the
front elevation is fully demountable
to allow aircraft to be brought in
and removed.

Right: The roof had to span 90 metres
and be strong enough to suspend a
number of aircraft from the soffit.

Right: The roof was supported on an in-situ concrete ring beam above a continuous band of glazing.

Below: A Lockheed SR-71 Blackbird strategic reconnaissance aircraft.

The B52 was a monster: 49 metres long, with a wingspan of 61 metres, it weighed 83,000 kilograms and was capable of carrying a 32,000-kilogram payload. In 1995, Norman Foster managed to cage one.

The American Air Museum at Duxford in Cambridgeshire was a supersized children's mobile, with aircraft as heavy as 10 tonnes suspended from the exposed-concrete soffit. And not only did the roof have to be immensely strong, it also had to span 90 metres in order to house the star exhibit: the Vietnam War–era B52. "The underside of the roof canopy provides a calm and distraction-free background to the exhibition area", wrote project architect Simon Reed and engineer Kevin Franklin in *Concrete Quarterly*, ignoring the fact that nervous visitors might be staring upwards trying to work out how the whole thing didn't cave in.[9]

The roof's shape was based on a small section of a torus—essentially a ring doughnut. This gave it curves in two directions: one, transversely, based on a 64-metre radius, the other a gentler 278-metre radius as the 100-metre-long structure sloped from front to back, gradually merging into the flat Cambridgeshire airfield. The shell was 1-metre deep and constructed from two 100-millimetre thick precast concrete slabs, stiffened by a series of precast ribs. The complex geometry required the slabs to be broken down into a range of smaller units: the lower shell comprised 268 panels, 72 of which were individually shaped, while the rest used one of six steel moulds; the upper shell was 754 far smaller units, most of which came from one of five moulds. The 278-metre longitudinal radius resulted in such a slight curve that the panels could be cast flat lengthwise, resulting in an undetectably faceted surface.

The roof was supported on an in-situ concrete ring beam, beneath which a continuous band of glazing wrapped around the building—giving the impression that 6,000 tonnes of concrete were somehow floating above the substructure. In reality, 34 supporting steel arms, set behind the glazing, drew all the forces from the roof down to a second ring beam and on through the in-situ concrete A-frame abutments into the ground-bearing slab. This enabled the front of the building to be filled with a fully demountable structural glass wall: a means for getting the aircraft in and out, as well as a diorama of the aerial display within.

UNESCO
Meditation Centre
Paris, France
Tadao Ando

Issue 179, Summer 1996

Opposite: Light is drawn into the stark interior through a narrow gap between the walls and roof.

Left: The Meditation Centre viewed from UNESCO's other concrete masterpiece, the 1958 Congress Hall.

Below: Each concrete panel is defined by Ando's trademark arrangement of six boltholes.

Few people stirred as much excitement at 1990s *Concrete Quarterly* as Tadao Ando. Here was an architect unflinching in his choice of unadorned concrete and lauded for it throughout the world. Suddenly everyone was discussing the 'purity' of concrete and dashing to Osaka to pay homage. He even had a dog called Corbusier. Did this mean that concrete modernism was back in favour?

Not exactly, decided columnist Dennis Sharp after his own pilgrimage to Japan in 1995. Ando's impeccable fair-faced concrete—"smooth as silk"—was less a declaration of structural honesty, more a "dramatic effect".[10] His simple geometric forms were as much light as material, usually illuminated by narrow openings in the thick-cast concrete. Perhaps the most famous example is the 1989 Church of Light in Ibaraki, where a slender cross slices the east wall into four, its stark lines of light the only suggestion of interior decoration.

In 1996, fresh from winning the Pritzker Architecture Prize, Ando travelled to France for the opening of what was only his fourth European project, the UNESCO Meditation Centre, which the organisation had commissioned in the shadow of its other concrete masterpiece: the 1958 headquarters complex designed by Marcel Breuer, Pier Luigi Nervi and Bernard Zehrfuss. Writing in *Concrete Quarterly*, journalist Ian Phillips described the addition as "trademark" Ando. Concrete panels, each with his customary six boltholes, formed a simple cylindrical shape, while a narrow gap between the walls and roof drew light into the otherwise sealed form. A shallow pond—water being another recurring Ando theme—suggested tranquillity. "The whole thing is decidedly Zen", thought Phillips.[11]

There is always an edge to the serenity of Ando's buildings, however. As he explained in his 1997 Royal Medal Address, when in the late 1960s he first decided to become an architect, he "always had firmly in [his] mind the state of Japan after the war".[12] The Meditation Centre had a very personal meaning for an architect who had been brought up amid the destruction of Osaka. Stones exposed to the Hiroshima bomb were embedded in the floor, casting the concrete above in the role of a solemn, anonymous witness to history. "I wanted to express nothingness", Ando claimed, "and to create a space in which, once inside, people feel how ridiculous it is to fight among themselves."[13]

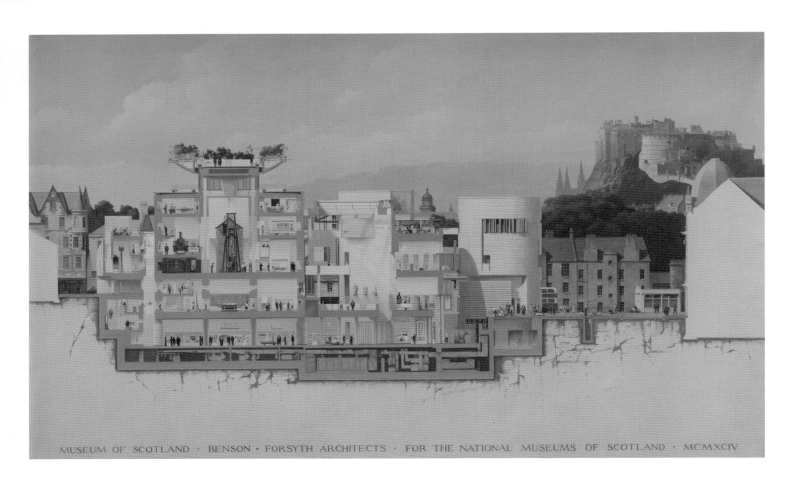

MUSEUM OF SCOTLAND · BENSON · FORSYTH ARCHITECTS · FOR THE NATIONAL MUSEUMS OF SCOTLAND · MCMXCIV

National Museum of Scotland
Edinburgh, UK
Benson + Forsyth,
Anthony Hunt Associates

Issue 185, Winter 1997

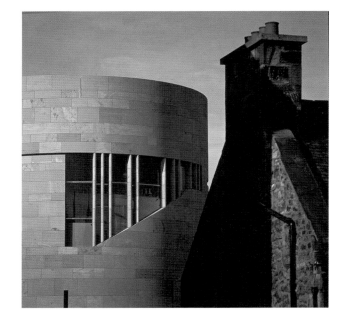

Above: Oil painting by Carl Laubin
showing a section through the museum.

Right: Externally, the concrete walls
were clad in local Clashach sandstone.

Below: The cantilever of the boat-like curved roof was formed in in-situ white concrete.

Right: The roof runs the length of the main gallery and also supports a roof terrace.

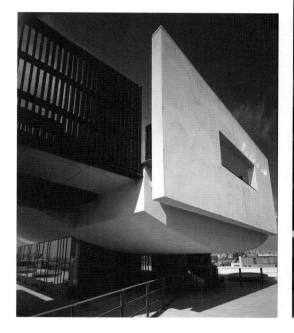

The National Museum of Scotland in Edinburgh was the last major public building of the millennium to be built north of the border, and the first to be completed in the heady atmosphere of devolution. The brief had demanded a building capable of placing Scotland's twentieth-century architecture on an international stage, "to stand testimony to the culture of our time", as project architect Peter Wilson, from local practice Benson + Forsyth, put it.[14] It was also an opportunity to show off Scottish architects on an international stage—at a time when the competition for the National Parliament Building was being whittled down to a decidedly non-Scottish shortlist.

In the winter of 1997, as the six-storey castle-like building was nearing completion, Wilson gave *Concrete Quarterly* a sneak preview. The concrete frame and walls had been rising quickly on the prominent Old Town site for the preceding 20 months but what passers-by could not see was the "exquisite quality of the cathedral-grade fair-faced in-situ concrete and the finely finished precast stairs within". Structural engineer Anthony Hunt Associates, meanwhile, had created "breath-taking cantilevers and concrete walls appearing to hang in space without visible means of support".

The museum was to offer a history of Scotland from early man to the present day, with exhibits ranging from Mary Queen of Scots' earrings to a full-size cruck frame house. Unusually for a modern museum, Benson + Forsyth designed the interior around the exhibits, leading to an intricate layout—some described it as labyrinthine. As a result, concrete was used not just for the frame but for built-in display cases and smaller discrete galleries.

Wilson treated the interior concrete as if it were an exhibit in itself, offering the visitor a "new impression of [the material] and its potential as a finished surface". The colour of the concrete had been achieved by mixing normal aggregate with white cement and white Ballidon sand; the exceptionally smooth finish resulted from the careful application of sealant and shutter-release agents onto the birch-faced ply surface of the formwork. "The material's finished quality provides an eloquent demonstration of Louis Kahn's description of concrete as the marble of the twentieth century", Wilson wrote—a sentiment that hadn't been voiced for a while in Britain.

Externally the concrete walls were mainly clad in striations of locally quarried Clashach sandstone, emphasising the parallels with Edinburgh Castle, brooding away above the Old Town. But the white concrete was visible on the precast copings and the framing to the rendered panels of the south elevation. It also formed the spectacular in-situ cantilever of the curved roof, which ran like a boat's hull above the main gallery and supported a roof terrace—a unique vantage point for looking out over Edinburgh and watching the new Scotland emerge.

1 Pringle, John, "Expression of Quality", *Concrete Quarterly*, Issue 174, Autumn 1992, p 4.

2 Outram, John, "An Artificial Form That Need Not Be Limited to Mimicry", *Concrete Quarterly*, Issue 178, Spring 1996, p 8.

3 Glancey, Jonathan, "Classical Precaster", *Concrete Quarterly*, Issue 165, Summer 1990, pp 2–5. All subsequent quotations in this section are from this piece.

4 Pringle, John, "Expression of Quality", *Concrete Quarterly*, Issue 174, Autumn 1992, pp 2–5. All subsequent quotations in this section are from this piece.

5 Campbell, Betty, "Editorial", *Concrete Quarterly*, Issue 5, Spring 1949, p 1.

6 McGuckin, Stephen, "Waterloo International", *Concrete Quarterly*, Issue 176, Spring 1993, pp 18–20. All subsequent quotations in this section are from this piece.

7 Furman, Adam Nathaniel, "Ghosts of a Future Past", *Icon*, Issue 167, May 2017, p 43.

8 Takasaki, Masaharu, "Spirit of Place", *Concrete Quarterly*, Issue 176, Spring 1993, pp 26–27. All subsequent quotations in this section are from this piece.

9 Reed, Simon and Franklin, Kevin, "Flight into the Realms of Strength and Efficiency", *Concrete Quarterly*, Issue 177, Winter 1995, p 6.

10 Sharp, Dennis, "Sharp Angles", *Concrete Quarterly*, Issue 182, Spring 1997, p 15.

11 Phillips, Ian, "Japan's Architect of Geometry and Tranquillity", *Concrete Quarterly*, Issue 179, Summer 1996, p 5.

12 "Tadao Ando's Royal Medal Address", *Concrete Quarterly*, Issue 184, Autumn 1997, p 3.

13 Phillips, "Japan's Architect of Geometry and Tranquillity", p 5.

14 Wilson, Peter, "Concrete – The Marble of the Twentieth

15 Century", *Concrete Quarterly*, Issue 185, Winter 1997, pp 8–11. All subsequent quotations in this section are from this piece.

y Community Centre
uomey and Casey O'Rourke
d
mmer 2009

By the turn of the millennium, there was a renewed confidence to architecture, emboldened by a buoyant economy and the possibilities of digital design, and encapsulated by the ubiquitous term 'iconic'. Frank Gehry's Guggenheim Museum in Bilbao, completed in 1997, had set a template for using cultural buildings of bold, original design to resuscitate Europe's post-industrial edgelands. Over the following decade, cities from Marseille to Salford would turn to the architectural community in the hope of repeating the trick.

Of course, a city didn't have to be impoverished to seek an iconic cultural building. Perhaps the most spectacular museum of the decade was the Phaeno Science Centre in Wolfsburg, one of Germany's richest cities, where Zaha Hadid performed the same freeform gymnastics with structure as Gehry had with cladding at Bilbao. And nor did an icon have to be a cultural building: Santiago Calatrava's Turning Torso gave the Swedish city of Malmö 150 luxury apartments as well as a world-famous landmark.

If this all sounds slightly frivolous, particularly in the context of the ensuing era of global economic austerity, then there was also an underlying seriousness to the architecture of the 2000s. Architects may have occasionally displayed the bravado of the 1960s but it was tempered by many of the same anxieties that blighted the 1970s. The 'iconic' trend was part of a wider debate about making city centres more habitable, after decades during which they had been systematically emptied of life. As in the 1970s, when concrete assumed a new role in the vanguard of pedestrianisation, now it was being used to create large landscaped spaces in the heart of cities. In Barcelona's South Eastern Coastal Park, for example, Foreign Office Architects turned 50,000 square metres of reclaimed land into an esplanade of moon-shaped concrete tiles.

There was, of course, one overriding preoccupation for building designers as the decade wore on: the dawning realisation that the climate was getting hotter, and we needed to burn far, far less fossil fuel if we had any hope of slowing the change down. This had a huge effect on concrete: both in the way that it was used and the way that it was made. In the UK, architects such as Bennetts Associates and Feilden Clegg Bradley led the way in exploiting the material's thermal mass, particularly in public and commercial buildings, as a means of reducing the need for energy-hungry air-conditioning. Suddenly, exposed concrete walls and ceilings weren't so much an expressed structure as an expressed sustainability strategy. There was also a renewed impetus to use strengthening techniques such as post-tensioning, as the less material that was needed to create a solid structure, the less energy was embodied in its construction.

At the same time, research into concrete mixes took on an added urgency. With the production of cement the most carbon-intensive aspect of concrete, producers began to explore alternative binding materials. Aukett Fitzroy Robinson's Adnams Distribution Centre in Reydon, Suffolk, captured the new 'back to nature' spirit by using a hemp-based concrete, together with lime-based building blocks, for its walls. But more common were industrial by-products such as fly ash and ground granulated blast-furnace slag, which not only reduced a building's carbon footprint, but also altered the tone of the finish. Climate change was becoming a new aesthetic force in architecture.

Market Place Theatre
and Arts Centre
Armagh, UK
Glenn Howells Architects

Issue 197, Winter 2000

Above: A light-coloured concrete
mix was specified to match the
local limestone.

Right: Louvres cast into the roof draw
light deep into the building.

Opposite: Care was taken to line up
the joints in the columns and roof
panels precisely.

It is the architectural world's version of alchemy: take the base ingredients of aggregate and cement and try to turn them back into stone. By the turn of the millennium, precast manufacturers were getting pretty close.

The Market Place Theatre and Arts Centre in Armagh is a fine example of the precaster's art. Tucked into a steep site in the civic heart of the city, the building had to be a symbol of Armagh's modern cultural life while also deferring to the surrounding historic buildings, notably the mighty nineteenth-century St Patrick's Roman Catholic Cathedral, which loomed over it from the hill behind. Glenn Howells decided to build the theatre entirely from polished concrete, as if wall and roof, inside and outside, were a continuous surface. The architecture would be unmistakably modern, with its slender precast panels and columns, but the concrete would be specially fabricated to echo the characteristic Armagh limestone.

The concrete served another purpose too. Designers were beginning to seize on the material's thermal mass to reduce buildings' energy needs, and *Concrete Quarterly* was impressed by the way that the structure evened out the highs and lows of the auditorium's temperature. "This is a building that exemplifies all the positive attributes of concrete", the magazine concluded, "visual harmony with its surrounding environment, quality of aesthetic finish, attention to the smallest of details, and its use for environmental control."[1]

The concrete mix was developed through painstaking colour and texture matching against the local stone. Samples of materials were obtained from throughout Europe and tested for quality, performance and weathering, until finally Howells settled on an exotic mix of coarse Derby limestone and Spanish dolomite fines. The finish was so light as to be almost luminous, an effect heightened by the downlighters and luminaires precast into the panels of the entrance canopy.

The casting process for the roof panels proved particularly involved. In addition to a high-quality finish, the roof needed louvres, to draw indirect light into the foyer below, and integrated lighting, drainage and services—all within a shallow depth to maintain the building's elegant profile and modest scale in relation to its historic setting. The designers used computer visualisations and sun path models to develop a total of 57 prototype roofing panels.

The soffits were meticulously finished, first with a floor polisher fitted with diamond abrasive pads, and then a handheld pad to get into tight corners and joints. The uncompromising standard of detailing is evident on the outside too: the joints between the roof panels and the 350-millimetre-diameter columns line up perfectly, creating the impression of a seamless fusion of elements.

Simmons Hall
Boston, US
Steven Holl

Issue 206, Winter 2003

Above: Hall designed the structure to be "porous and permeable", with several large sections cut out.

Right: The small square windows are arranged in three rows per floor, creating the illusion that the building is 30 storeys tall.

Right: The interior is arranged around six amorphous multi-storey spaces made from in-situ concrete.

Below: The concrete walls and staircases have an impeccable board-marked finish.

The Boston suburb of Cambridge is home to some of the finest concrete buildings in the world, modern monuments by the likes of Le Corbusier, Walter Gropius and José Luís Sert. But by the end of the twentieth century, its reputation as the concrete capital of the US was starting to crack. Developers were turning increasingly to steel high-rises with, at most, thin layers of stone or brick cladding.

Which is why Steven Holl's Simmons Hall student housing block for the Massachusetts Institute of Technology (MIT) was something of an event in the concrete world. Here, wrote the architectural historian William Menking in *Concrete Quarterly*, was "a serious piece of architecture that is refreshing in the somewhat stuffy atmosphere of recent academic buildings and the blocks of postmodern dreck that scar all American cities".[2] It was also a large concrete building that seemed to revel in its scale: its defining external feature was the 58-centimetre square cut-out windows—5,538 of them—arranged in three rows per floor, giving the impression, if viewed from a distance, that the ten-storey building was actually three times bigger.

There was more than a hint of Brutalism about the massing of this exterior, which resembled "a concrete honeycomb", or as Menking was told by an MIT student, a "computer punch card". The building's shape included several cut-outs, like "two Pac-Man figures set head to head", which Holl argued made the block permeable, offering views through the structure to the distant Boston skyline and the Charles River. Menking suspected this was a bit of an overstatement: "It is still, after all, a large building, so it is unclear how residents behind the structure will be able to see through its form."

Menking also felt that Holl could have shown a little more faith in his structural material. The exterior precast concrete panels were clad in sanded aluminium and many of the square cut-outs were painted yellow, red or blue—a nod perhaps to Le Corbusier's Unité d'Habitation but also an act of concealment. "Holl seems unwilling to allow the concrete to carry the day", Menking wrote, "and constantly tones down the material to soften its rough and direct surfaces."

The interiors were a happier experience—a series of spaces that "could only happen with concrete":

> The most impressive are the six multi-storey group lounges that slice up, across and through, the standard residential floors. These flowing spaces, made of thin poured concrete, suggest Bilbao crossed with la Tourette and cut diagonally through the building's walls and floors, often spilling into the hallways.

The patterns left by the timber formwork were beautiful, Menking noted, but highlighted how a tradition had been all but lost during the years of "dreck". Despite Boston's modernist concrete heritage, the contractor struggled to find enough experts in concrete formwork to complete the structure, in the end having to bring older form-makers out of retirement. Menking hoped that Simmons Hall would prove the training ground for a new generation of concrete specialists—the start of something rather than just an echo of the city's former glories.

Phaeno Science Centre
Wolfsburg, Germany
Zaha Hadid Architects,
Adams Kara Taylor

Issue 208, Summer 2004

Above: Because of the sharp angles of the walls and the amount of reinforcement needed, a self-compacting concrete was specified.

Right: The 'cone' walls are inclined up to 45 degrees.

Right: To create a monolithic effect,
the vast planes of concrete were cast
without movement joints.

Below: The cones and the slabs depend
on each other for support; the whole
structure had to be propped until the
entire concourse slab had been poured.

No architect has graced the pages of *Concrete Quarterly* more often in the twenty-first century than Zaha Hadid. But then no architect did more to push concrete to the limits, combining beautifully fluid forms with what often seemed like a wilful disregard both for the laws of gravity and the sound sleep of structural engineers. The first Hadid project that the magazine covered in detail was the Phaeno Science Centre in Wolfsburg, Germany—a building that reflected the museum's scientific remit by apparently being summoned from another planet.

It was the type of building that added new words to the lexicon of structural engineering—not that mere words could quite do justice to the concepts in question. Hadid's idea was of a main exhibition floor space that "melted down" into ten reinforced-concrete structural "cones".[3] Except that cone wasn't quite the right term. Each was a different geometric shape, which shifted as it rose, and with surfaces inclined at 45 degrees, they blurred the boundary between walls and floor. Even the term 'structural' was a little imprecise, as they relied on the floor slab for restraint. Paul Scott, project engineer for Adams Kara Taylor (AKT), told *Concrete Quarterly*:

> Structurally they are not quite one thing, and not quite another. I suppose they are part arch and part beam, but we had to get away from the traditional idea of thinking of it in terms of structural elements and naming them.

The only way to approach the structural design was to treat it as a single entity and then analyse the whole building for gravity loads, thermal loads and shrinkage in one model.

But there was no correspondingly radical new method for constructing such a form: the best option was still to cast reinforced concrete in situ using hand-built timber formwork. AKT redefined the geometry of each cone so that they could be set out and built by the local carpenters: "Each was either a triangle or quadrilateral in plan with rounded corners of fixed radii", *Concrete Quarterly* explained. There were also irregular sliced openings in each cone that had to be negotiated—these were to house functions of the museum such as toilets, gift shop and auditorium:

> [AKT] designed the plane of each slice, then used Microstation [software] to define all the key points, such as the centre points and radii for each arc.... Once everyone was happy, this was translated into setting-out information, which was supplied by defining the angle of each cutting plane.

If this wasn't complicated enough, AKT also had to devise a system that enabled the steel fixers to work out where to put all the reinforcement—they needed an 'unfolded' version of the inside face of each cone. As AKT's Julian Birbeck put it: "We were collapsing the 3D world into 2D." The density of the reinforcement grid was immense, and this led to more pioneering in the material specification. Traditional vibration of the concrete would have been impossible due to the amount of steel and the irregularity of the angled walls, so the team used a self-compacting mix. This allowed pours of up to 8 metres and gave "a finish that would have been impossible to achieve through general construction techniques", said Scott. It would become a defining feature of Hadid projects over the years to come.

Thirteen years on, the project can be read as a landmark in getting the construction industry to work in three dimensions. With AKT, Hadid's team basically had to rethink many of the rules of construction, from the design of double-curved forms, to the way this information was presented to contractors, to the materials used. While designers of the previous generation such as Oscar Niemeyer and Gio Ponti had claimed that developments in concrete had freed them to think in new forms, Hadid turned this idea on its head. She imagined new forms and then worried about how to construct them.

Turning Torso
Malmö, Sweden
Santiago Calatrava

Issue 209, Autumn 2004

The tower was twice as high as any
other building in the city.

Righr: In total, the structure required more than 20,000 cubic metres of concrete. The central core was formed from in-situ concrete and packed with over 4,000 tonnes of reinforcement.

Far right: The tower appears to rotate 90 degrees as it rises.

'Biomimicry' was a buzzword of post-millennial architecture. Rapid advances in digital design gave architects free rein to propose more irregular, organic forms—and, crucially, gave engineers the tools to make them stand up. The early 2000s were also a time of deliberately iconic architecture. Excited by the effect that Frank Gehry's Guggenheim Museum had had on the fortunes of the post-industrial city of Bilbao, public authorities and private developers jostled to commission ever more exuberant buildings from a global elite of 'starchitects'.

These two trends collided spectacularly in the figure of Santiago Calatrava. If you were a town in want of a statement bridge or building in the early 2000s, Calatrava was the man you called. His designs were always organic in inspiration and invariably spectacular in execution. As in nature, the spectacle often derived from a functional element: the movable wing-like brise-soleil that soared over the Quadracci Pavilion in Milwaukee, for example, or the towering mast of the Alamillo Bridge in Seville. Calatrava, *Concrete Quarterly* wrote, "removes any boundaries between engineering, sculpture and architecture".[4]

In 2004, one of Calatrava's most wilfully expressive buildings was twisting skywards over the Swedish city of Malmö. The Turning Torso was a white aluminium-clad tower of luxury apartments that appeared to rotate 90 degrees as it rose. At 190 metres, it was twice as high as any other building in the harbour town. It was also, *Concrete Quarterly* noted, "the first residential high-rise tower meant to be seen as a free-standing sculptural element within the cityscape".[5]

The tower had begun life as a sculpture, an image of which had been submitted with Calatrava's entry in the 1999 competition for the Öresund Bridge between Sweden and Denmark. The sculpture explored the human body in motion—a man's torso twisted as far as it can naturally be pushed while staying directly upright. As *Concrete Quarterly* put it:

Think of the position you would take up to launch a frisbee while standing straight—aiming your missile horizontally, arms at shoulder height and swung round to ensure projectile delivery with as much power as possible—and you will be about there.

The sculpture was seen by Malmö-based developer Johnny Örbäck, who convinced Calatrava to design a residential building based on the concept.

The tower may have had a lithe, athletic form, but it required a massive, highly engineered structure to root it to the ground. In total, more than 20,000 cubic metres of concrete were deployed to perform Calatrava's twist. Resting on piles driven deep into a solid foundation of limestone bedrock 15 metres below ground level, a central core, formed from in-situ concrete, rose the height of the building. Its walls were 2.5 metres thick at the base, tapering to 0.4 metres at the highest level, and it was packed with over 4,000 tonnes of steel reinforcement. Around this core rotated nine irregular concrete cubes, stacked one on top of the other and twisting ten degrees from bottom to top. The concrete cubes contained five storeys and had an almost square floorplate with an additional triangular section reinforced by an external steel support. The structure rose one cube at a time in a two-month cycle—each floor consisting of a slab, a core wall, a corridor slab and the walls for elevators and stairs.

When *Concrete Quarterly* reported on the Turning Torso in autumn 2004, it was still under construction, but had already become a local landmark. "Reception for the startling, soaring form [was] slightly uneasy at first, but has rapidly changed as the building has progressed to one of astonished delight", the magazine wrote. Calatrava's Torso would soon become shorthand for its host city in tourist guides and a succession of 'Scandi noir' TV serials. Malmö had its Guggenheim.

New Street Square
London, UK
Bennetts Associates, Pell Frischmann
Issue 209, Autumn 2004

Above: The development has created a new open space in a dense part of the City of London.

Right: The concrete frames were expressed to give the scheme its own 'feel', distinct from typical City offices.

Opposite: The square can be used for public events.

Rab Bennetts has probably done more than any other British architect to banish the suspended ceiling from the modern workplace. As far back as 1991, he was explaining in *Concrete Quarterly* his reasons for expressing the structure of the new PowerGen Headquarters in Coventry:

> The mass of the structure, exposed to view in much the same way as the vaulted structures of pre-Victorian warehouses, facilitates natural ventilation through its thermal storage capacity: the profligacy of air-conditioning and the deadening effects of flat suspended ceilings have been avoided and the structure will resume its natural status as the means of providing shape and form to architectural space.[6]

In an era when sustainability was at best a vague aspiration, particularly in commercial office development, Bennetts was not only showing how a thermally massive structure could cut energy use, but also arguing for it as a desirable workplace aesthetic. This combination of commercial nous and forward-thinking sustainable design would eventually lead to one of the defining London office projects of the early 2000s.

New Street Square was a development of four towers ranging from six to nineteen storeys on a prime, if rather neglected, site between High Holborn and Fleet Street. The razor-sharp glass profile of the tallest building seemed to declare it a new destination in London's freshly branded 'Midtown', complete with pedestrian routes and, as the name suggested, a public square.

But *Concrete Quarterly* was rather more interested in what was going on behind the glass.

All four buildings were united by a strong concrete aesthetic: this was partly to give the scheme its own "feel", distinct from the 1980s generation of steel-frame high-rises that dominated the neighbouring City, and partly to meet stringent sustainability targets.[7] Again, Bennetts was ahead of the curve, understanding both that ensuring a development's long-term viability was in fact an environmental issue, and that the most sustainable way to use any material was to use as little of it as possible.

These two themes converged in New Street Square's use of post-tensioned concrete floor slabs—the focus of *Concrete Quarterly's* article. "Post-tensioned slabs are not new", it wrote, "but they are more common in the US, Australia and the Far East than the UK, which is now waking up to the technique's possibilities."[8] Essentially, post-tensioning involves running steel cables within the slab; once the concrete has been cast and gained sufficient strength, the cables are pulled tight by a high-powered jack, cut and then locked into place. They are flat, thin and strong, and dispense with the need for upstand and downstand beams. This minimises the building's height to such an extent that "it could mean an extra storey on a ten-storey building", said *Concrete Quarterly*. It also meant far less concrete was needed overall.

The other thing about post-tensioned floors is that they are easier to adapt than conventional concrete slabs. For one thing, it is fairly easy to punch through a thin, flat slab if you don't have to worry about the awkward mass of upstand beams. At New Street Square, the cables were also threaded through pipework filled

Opposite: Post-tensioning enabled the engineers to design thinner floor slabs, allowing a greater floor-to-ceiling ratio.

Right: The sharp profile of the development's tallest building has made the square a landmark for 'Midtown' on the western reaches of the City.

with grout under high pressure, which keeps the cables in tension even after they have been cut through. This makes the building "far more flexible during its occupation, and easier to recycle at the end of its life", *Concrete Quarterly* noted.

Flexibility mattered. New Street Square was one of many London office developments to be built over the grave of a 60s block that had been branded functional at the time but had quickly proved obsolete. Architects had simply not been able

to imagine how the nature of work was going to change. The new generation of offices couldn't afford to make the same mistake again. Even in the short period since New Street Square was completed, tenants' needs have already changed markedly, particularly with the rise of cloud computing and the commercial imperative to reduce carbon footprints. Bennetts did not try to predict the future; but his buildings can respond to the unknown. And perhaps there is nothing more sustainable than that.

The Darwin Centre
London, UK
CF Møller, Arup

Issue 226, Winter 2008

Above: The Cocoon is built within a glass atrium next to Alfred Waterhouse's ornate 1881 museum.

Right: The windowless pod is an enigmatic presence.

Opposite left: The curving form is the largest sprayed concrete structure in Europe.

Opposite right: Inside, the concrete is left exposed to create a cave-like exhibition space.

In 2008 the Natural History Museum acquired a strange new exhibit. Almost touching the sides of its vast glazed display cabinet, the bulging Cocoon was as outsized in its context as the famous blue whale and diplodocus in the neighbouring galleries.

Except, of course, the Cocoon wasn't an exhibit; it was a £78 million exhibition space, archive and laboratory for the museum's collection of insects and plants, and the centrepiece of the museum's new Darwin Centre. Its design was in stark contrast to the ornately Gothic 1881 museum by Alfred Waterhouse. Whereas Waterhouse's intricate terracotta facades, inhabited by sculptures of exotic plants and animals, "expressed the diversity of the collections inside", CF Møller's windowless pod was simply enigmatic—who knew what was about to hatch out?[9]

The Cocoon was also, at eight storeys high and 65 metres long, Europe's largest sprayed concrete structure. Spraying concrete had gained in popularity in the age of digital design as a means of creating apparently freeform structures without having to use formwork; instead the mix was hosed onto curved reinforcement bars or mesh. At the Darwin Centre, the immense bulging wall was set out by marking 3D co-ordinates generated by Rhino computer software onto scaffolding. These were then used to position reinforcement bars, behind which was placed an expanded metal mesh to give a keying surface for the concrete. To "fine tune the shape", a top layer of concrete was dry-sprayed (which meant that water was only added at the nozzle), then hand-trowelled.

The surface was finished with a polished plaster made from aged lime putty and Bianco Carrara marble. This had "a tone and lustre similar to that of the cobalt blue terracotta bands in the Waterhouse's facades". The 3,500-square-metre surface had to include a number of expansion joints to avoid cracking, but these were carefully set out to extend the biomorphic metaphor, appearing as "threads wrapping round the Cocoon".

Inside was a cave-like exhibition space with a ramp winding down through three floors. Here, the concrete was left exposed and finished with mineral paint. The monolithic structure held another advantage: devoid of nooks or crannies, there was nowhere for the biggest threat to the collection to thrive. This was the aptly named museum beetle (*Anthrenus museorum*), which apparently has a taste for dried specimens and textiles. Not all insects, it seems, were welcome at the Darwin Centre.

2000–2009

Neues Museum
Berlin, Germany
David Chipperfield Architects,
Julian Harrap Architects

Issue 227, Spring 2009

The grand central staircase was rebuilt
in precast concrete following the form
of the original.

Left: A lattice structure of concrete beams and slender 24-metre-high columns was inserted in the Egyptian Courtyard.

Below: The concrete frame helps to define different spaces within the gallery.

In 2008, David Chipperfield completed an 11-year project that overturned conventional wisdom about restoration and the relationship between new architecture and the past. And the material he chose to mediate between these layers of time was precast concrete.

The Neues Museum was designed by Friedrich August Stüler and completed in 1859, the second of five monumental museums of art and archaeology to be built on an island in the Spree river in central Berlin. Bombing raids in 1943 and 1945 destroyed large parts of the fabric, and it was subsequently left to rot until the East German government began a restoration project in the mid-1980s. The fall of the Berlin Wall brought a halt to proceedings until, in 1997, Chipperfield was charged with bringing the building back to life.

Chipperfield's groundbreaking approach was neither to restore the building to its former glory nor to start again, but instead to retain the beauty of the ruin he found and insert new elements only where appropriate. "The new and the old reinforce each other; not in a desire for contrast, but in a search for continuity", he later explained. "We have created a new building from the remains of the old, not celebrating or hiding its history, but including it."[10]

With conservation specialist Julian Harrap, Chipperfield began by assessing the surviving fabric. The architectural response differed on a room-by-room basis, depending on the conditions they found: in some places, it was merely a case of repairing fire-scorched columns; in others whole galleries needed to be inserted. Throughout, precast concrete acted as the bridge between old and new, "fusing the shattered parts into a comprehensible whole", as Concrete Quarterly put it.[11]

Chipperfield wanted to avoid using concrete simply as a "fragile" filler. "In some areas [it] has been used in a neutral way but in others has been allowed a strong physical presence of its own", wrote Concrete Quarterly. The most emphatic interventions were needed in some of the museum's most prominent spaces. In the once-lavish Egyptian Courtyard, only two of the original walls remained. The other two were reconstructed in reclaimed brick to match, and within the space Chipperfield inserted a lattice structure of concrete beams supported on ten slender 24-metre-high concrete columns with a glass roof above. The move "both emphasises the height of the room and defines more intimate spaces within it", Concrete Quarterly noted. The grand central staircase, meanwhile, was rebuilt following the form if not the detail of the original, stripped down "in huge precast concrete blocks that bear on one another in a way that is reminiscent of Egyptian architecture".

The detailing of the concrete was exemplary throughout. The precast columns and basement wall linings were given a rough, matt texture that toned with the reclaimed brickwork, while other elements had a more refined polished finish. In places the aggregate was used in a larger than normal 32-millimetre grade so its distinctive swirling veins were visible. Joints of just 5 millimetres were specified between the precast elements, the largest of which measured 10 by 4 metres, which meant that fabrication had to be extremely accurate. The metal shutters were carefully cleaned and recalibrated after each pour to achieve a tolerance of +/- 1 millimetre in any dimension.

The uniform light colour was the product of sand, white cement and marble aggregate from the Erzgebirge Mountains. "The mix is greater than the sum of its parts", said project director Alexander Schwarz. "On one hand it needs to be neutral but on the other it must have some character of its own." Perhaps only concrete could have performed such a nuanced role: weaving itself into the multilayered history of a building, while also creating something completely new.

2000–2009

Sean O'Casey Community Centre
Dublin, Ireland
O'Donnell + Tuomey,
Casey O'Rourke

Issue 228, Summer 2009

The community centre rises above the
terraced houses of Dublin's docks.

Below: It was designed as a
series of discrete spaces around
four courtyards.

Right: Circular rooflights emphasise
the solidity of the concrete structure
and add a playful touch.

With the Sean O'Casey Community Centre, Irish practice O'Donnell + Tuomey tried hard not to build an icon. The building was to contain a 150-seat theatre, a sports hall, a crèche and daycare facilities for the elderly, and its design was a careful, considered exercise in separating these functions while providing oblique connections and views between them via a series of courtyards— an old-fashioned sense of community, in other words.

But the centre was more than a functional building; it also had to be a visible symbol of the regeneration of East Wall, the former Dublin docking community that claimed playwright O'Casey as its most famous son. At €7.9 million (£6.5 million) for a 2,080-square-metre building, it represented a serious investment by the Dublin Docklands Development Authority, "particularly when you think of the cheap and not-so-cheerful buildings community centres normally inhabit", noted *Concrete Quarterly's* Graham Bizley.[12]

O'Donnell + Tuomey took a far more subtle approach than many architects faced with similar briefs on the post-industrial fringes of European cities. Certainly there were the quirky circular windows, "scattered playfully" across the elevations. But the use of exposed ribbed concrete on all the external walls, echoing the silos and warehouses that once characterised the dockland landscape, created a slightly melancholic air. The five-storey block on one corner of the site was a more assertive

statement, but it was only included because the community wanted a tower. "They said: 'Everyone else has got one'", Tuomey later recalled.[13]

But the East Wall residents got far more than a tower. The Sean O'Casey Community Centre was a skilfully crafted building that made clever use of in-situ concrete to give it a robust—but never showy—presence on the docklands' terraced streets. The ribbed pattern, for example, was created by fixing corrugated galvanised steel sheets from the local builder's merchant to the inside of standard plywood shutters.

This rather primitive solution called for a degree of finessing. Pressure-washing the concrete would have ruined the ribbed profile, so it had to be sanded by hand to create a suitably smooth finish. Day joints were difficult to form neatly in the corrugated formwork so flat sections were introduced; again, these were rubbed down once the formwork was struck. Bizley liked the result: "These recesses introduce another layer of proportion to the facades and give the ribbed areas a more crafted feel."

The Sean O'Casey Centre, he concluded, "has succeeded in providing a symbol of the regeneration of the whole district". It also showed that such symbols could be achieved through intelligent design and attention to detail, and not just flashy gestures.

Bocconi University
Milan, Italy
Grafton Architects,
Studio Ingegneria E Pereira

Issue 229, Autumn 2009

Above: The architects wanted
the concrete to be as smooth as
possible and free from air bubbles.

Right: The lecture hall
cantilevers dramatically over
the long external piazza.

Opposite top: "A structure holding
the space".

Opposite bottom: The cantilevering
volumes form a variety of external and
internal street-like spaces.

Opposite right: The main concrete
staircase makes a dramatic statement
behind the 6.7-metre-high glass wall.

In 2008, Dublin-based Grafton Architects won the top prize at the inaugural World Architecture Festival with the sort of emphatic concrete structure that some assumed had died out 30 years before. The new building for Bocconi University in Milan may have been clad in grey marble, but the way that it "fractured and rose in a shifting composition of cantilevering forms" could only have been achieved in one material.[14]

This was architecture on a grand civic scale, its interior spaces described in terms of rural or urban landscape. Immediately inside the main entrance was a vast public foyer inspired by the *broletto*, a typical northern Italian town hall with an open colonnade marketplace. Grafton director Shelley McNamara imagined this as "a place of exchange, a filter between the university and the city". Above stretched a sky of glass-clad offices, interspersed with light wells to allow the sun to penetrate deep into the plan. Below ran a huge open concourse, a "magical subterranean realm", in the words of the World Architecture Festival judges. And dominating one corner of the plan was what McNamara called the "embedded boulder" of the 1,000-seat lecture hall.

For *Concrete Quarterly*, the building's "remarkable presence and sculptural quality" was testament to its ingenious structure, which contained more than 80,000 cubic metres of concrete but seemed to have barely any vertical support. The building was divided into five 24-metre clear-span bays; these were separated by a 3.4-metre "structural zone" with 1.2-metre-thick concrete fin-walls. The offices were suspended over the ground floor on steel tension cables from giant 24-metre-long concrete roof beams, while the floor slabs below were made from prestressed concrete to achieve the long spans.

The most complex structural solution was reserved for the boulder-like lecture hall, where the raked seating cantilevered several metres over a long external piazza. The sloping reinforced concrete floor slab was 600 millimetres thick and spanned the 24-metre bay. It was supported and counterbalanced by 400-millimetre-thick side walls and a 4-metre-deep beam that acted as the hall's rear wall. The cantilever was, *Concrete Quarterly* felt, "worthy of the heroic period of Modernism".

In contrast to their brutalist forebears, however, any mention of Brutalism, the architects demanded that the visible concrete be as smooth as possible and free from air bubbles. Forty-two mixes were tested and an entirely new pouring technique was developed "using a funnel pipe which delivers the concrete direct to the bottom of the formwork, preventing splashing". To ensure uniformity, every single mixer of concrete was tested when it arrived on site.

There could be no denying that this was assertive concrete architecture on a scale rarely seen since the 1960s. But half a century had brought a shift in perspective. Bocconi was no monolith; it was more "a structure holding the space"—as Grafton would describe a later project.[15] It was this permeability that *Concrete Quarterly* found so admirable: "The plastic qualities of concrete have given the university a new symbolic presence in the city, a fusion of permanence, movement and openness."

1   "Concrete Society Awards 2000/01", Issue 197, Winter 2000, formerly on concretequarterly.com and published by the British Cement Association, now available in The Concrete Society archives.

2   Menking, William, "Holl Picks Holes in Masonry Tradition", *Concrete Quarterly*, Issue 203, Winter 2003, pp 4–6. All subsequent quotations in this section are from the same article.

3   Cole, Margo, "Simple Answers to Museum Complexity", *Concrete Quarterly*, Issue 208, Summer 2004, pp 4–7. All subsequent quotations in this section are from the same article.

4   "Portrait of a Masterpiece", *Concrete Quarterly*, Issue 221, Autumn 2007, p 8.

5   "Turning Torso Twists New Life into Cubism", *Concrete Quarterly*, Issue 209, Autumn 2004, pp 4–7. All subsequent quotations in this section are from the same article.

6   Bennetts, Rab, "Space Frame", *Concrete Quarterly*, Issue 171, Winter 1991, p 4.

7   Bennetts Associates, *Five Insights*, London: Artifice, 2016, p 202.

8   Littlefield, David, "Thin Floors Create Roomy, Flexible Offices", *Concrete Quarterly*, Issue 217, Autumn 2006, pp 8–11. All subsequent quotations in this section are from the same article.

9   Bizley, Graham, "Venturing into the Cocoon", *Concrete Quarterly*, Issue 226, Winter 2008, pp 12–13. All subsequent quotations in this section are from the same article.

10 Rattenbury, Kester, "Neues Museum by David Chipperfield Architects in collaboration with Julian Harrap Architects", 30 September 2010, www.architectsjournal.co.uk/home/neues-museum-by-david-chipperfield-architects-in-collaboration-with-julian-harrap-architects/8606438.article.

11 Bizley, Graham, "Bringing a Smooth Finish to a Turbulent History", *Concrete Quarterly*, Issue 227, pp 4–7. All subsequent quotations in this section are from the same article.

12 Bizley, Graham, "The Ripple Effect Comes to Dublin", *Concrete Quarterly*, Issue 228, Summer 2009, pp 6–9. All subsequent quotations in this section are from the same article unless otherwise stated.

13 Rattenbury, Kester, "Sean O'Casey Community Centre by O'Donnell + Tuomey, Dublin, Ireland", 1 May 2009, www.architectural-review.com/today/sean-ocasey-community-centre-by-odonnell-tuomey-dublin-ireland/8601177.article.

14 Bizley, Graham, "Gateway to Education", *Concrete Quarterly*, Issue 229, Autumn 2009, pp 10–11. All subsequent quotations in this section are from the same article unless otherwise stated.

15 "The North Face of UTEC", *Concrete Quarterly*, Issue 259, Spring 2017, p 11.

2010–2017

Park Hill Phase One
Sheffield, UK
Hawkins\Brown,
Studio Egret West
Issue 238, Winter 2011

Since 2010, five of the seven winners of the Stirling Prize have been made from concrete. And not discreet concrete, doing its solid, structural job behind crowd-pleasing timber or brick cladding. This is beautiful, exposed, frankly inescapable concrete.

The architects and engineers of these buildings are the heirs of Pier Luigi Nervi, Félix Candela, Oscar Niemeyer, Ove Arup and many others, working within a tradition but taking it in completely new directions. There is the restrained late modernism of Stanton Williams' Sainsbury Laboratory in Cambridge—a National Theatre of science that nobody could describe as brutal. Or the virtuosic Zaha Hadid projects—Rome's MAXXI Museum[1] and the Evelyn Grace Academy in London (not to mention the London 2012 Aquatics Centre, featured here)—that revel in concrete's plasticity half a century after Gio Ponti had declared us liberated from the right angle.[2]

Then there's the Everyman Theatre, where Haworth Tompkins' controlled, board-marked concrete defines a free-spirited, 'everyman' material palette, in part a modern translation of the class-defying design language employed by Peter Moro at Nottingham Playhouse. And most recently, Burntwood School, where Allford Hall Monaghan Morris (AHMM) channelled

Marcel Breuer to reveal the beauty secreted in repeated precast forms.

One thing that all these projects have in common is that their designers express concrete not out of loyal adherence to modernist doctrine; they do it because they are confident that it looks good. Concrete's colour and texture are easier to control than ever. It can be pigmented, such as at David Chipperfield's purple-tinged Hepworth Gallery in West Yorkshire.[3] It can be ribbed, rippled, striped or sculpted, all of which are on show at Thomas Heatherwick's Nanyang Learning Hub in Singapore.[4] Or it can be simply left as struck, by architects confident in the tactile and aesthetic quality of their chosen concrete mix.

Of course, once clients are convinced that concrete is a desirable surface finish, the material's other qualities suddenly become more obvious. It is clearly a sensible choice for a school like Burntwood, able as it is to withstand the noise and impact of hundreds of children on a daily basis. Or for an Olympic diving board, which needs to cantilever like Fallingwater while maintaining an exact distance from the water below. Or even for hardwearing kitchen worktops and polished floors in designer homes. Concrete's reach in the second decade of the twenty-first century goes a long way.

As concrete has become more popular, so too have older buildings—so reviled in the 1980s—made a comeback. Denys Lasdun's National Theatre has been expertly refurbished by Haworth Tompkins, its board-marked walls and columns as fresh now as when they were first cast. And Park Hill, Sheffield City Council's glowering, hilltop housing estate, has been reimagined as apartments and workspaces for twenty-first-century design connoisseurs, complete with iPod-style cladding.

It is tempting to say that concrete has come full circle, but our uses for the material continue to evolve. As fears over climate change and energy resources intensify, its ability to act as a passive means of controlling temperature is coming to the fore. At the same time, its inherent plasticity has given it a central role in our nascent era of 3D printing and robotic construction. It is 60 years since Nervi described concrete as a "living creature", but it is still growing in new and unexpected ways.[5]

Sainsbury Laboratory
Cambridge, UK
Stanton Williams,
Adams Kara Taylor

Issue 233, Autumn 2010

Above: The laboratory was conceived
as a "series of geological strata"
amid the greenery of Cambridge's
Botanical Garden.

Right: Concrete is paired with
oak internally.

Left: The building provides world-class facilities for the study of plant development.

Below: Internal windows offer glimpses into the laboratories.

With the Stirling Prize-winning Sainsbury Laboratory, Stanton Williams showed that fair-faced concrete was now publicly acceptable just about anywhere. The laboratory, a research facility for the study of plant development, was in a hugely sensitive location: the University of Cambridge's 40-acre Botanic Garden, originally designed in 1831 by John Henslow, a mentor of Charles Darwin. It had to become part of this curated landscape, but it also had to be one of the University's showpiece buildings. As Alan Stanton, director of Stanton Williams, explained:

> The Sainsbury Laboratory is not only a new building, it's a new institution. We were challenged to produce a building of world-class quality that would attract scientists from all over the world.[6]

The architects responded with what *Concrete Quarterly* described as "a robust, classically proportioned two-storey building [with] a monolithic presence".[7] If the classical was alluded to by the rhythmic facade of slender limestone columns, the monolithic was supplied by expanses of perfectly controlled, light-coloured in-situ concrete. The specification was a scientific endeavour in its own right, the team building a 'Stonehenge' of huge test blocks to analyse the material's performance and ensure that they could achieve the same finish consistently. When it came to casting on site, shuttering boards were strictly laid out to conceal the joints between different pours, and the team went to great lengths to make sure there were no visible downstand beams, bolts or fixings. As a result, smooth expanses of uniform concrete appeared in jointless runs of up to 70 metres.

The other remarkable thing about the concrete at the Sainsbury Laboratory is how well it works with other materials. Writing in *Concrete Quarterly* in 2014, Stanton explained how many of the architects he admired have lifted people's perceptions of concrete by pairing it with luxurious materials. "The person who does this best is the great Italian architect Carlo Scarpa", he wrote.

> I recently visited his Gavina showroom in Bologna, which is in rough board-marked concrete with two big circular windows. There are grooves in the concrete where he's put gold leaf, and little bronze fittings around the windows—it ennobles the concrete, if that's not too grand a word.[8]

At the Sainsbury Laboratory, the concrete was paired with oak internally and layered with Metz limestone on the facades. "It's conceived almost as a series of geological strata, as if it's carved into the landscape—a layer of stone, a layer of concrete, a layer of stone", wrote Stanton. "By putting this very high-quality fair-faced concrete with a rather beautiful limestone and timber and beautiful detailing, it just became a very, very special material."

Park Hill Phase One
Sheffield, UK
Hawkins\Brown,
Studio Egret West

Issue 238, Winter 2011

Above: Hawkins\Brown altered the facades so that they were two-thirds glazed, with the remainder clad in bright colours.

Right: With its hilltop location, Park Hill provides a dramatic landmark for Sheffield.

Below: The 'streets in the sky' were criticised for their low ceilings, but have become an iconic feature of the estate.

Right: A mirror-finished helical stair offers a more welcoming entrance to the block.

At some point in the early 2000s, something changed in the public's relationship with Brutalism. Having been almost universally derided for much of the preceding 30 years, brutalist buildings seemed suddenly to have become (to choose a simile at random) much-loved friends with impeccably carbuncle-free noses.

For some, they had the aura of a perceived golden age of the Welfare State; to others, growing up in a time of mass obsolescence, their monumental, sculptured forms offered an appealing sense of solidity; some people just liked the way they looked in online photos. But whatever the reasons, the canny and historically literate developer Urban Splash chose a good moment to wake one of the great beasts of British Brutalism: Sheffield's Park Hill Estate.

Designed in 1957 by Jack Lynn and Ivor Smith of Sheffield City Architects Department, Park Hill was the most ambitious inner city housing development of its time. It was the first built project to use so-called 'streets in the air'—broad access decks named after the site's original back-to-back roads and partly inspired by the miners' terraces of Lynn's native North Seaton. "It aimed to facilitate the sort of neighbourliness that exists in a street on the ground where there is a choice of neighbours, room to stand and chat, and space for children to play", Smith recalled in 2008.[9] Other aspects of the design were also intended to engender a village-like atmosphere: flats and maisonettes were arranged in various permutations, and there were pubs by each of the lifts.

Park Hill was initially popular with residents, but during the 1980s the collapse of the steel industry hastened its decline, the building fabric began to deteriorate and the estate started to epitomise all the supposed ills of mass housing. There were even tales of air rifle snipers shooting at children in the school playground.[10] Despite that, it held on to a kind of iconic status, helped by its imposing location on the crest of a hill overlooking

the city. In 1998, a turning point came when English Heritage controversially granted it Grade II*-listed status, making it the largest listed structure in Europe.

This paved the way for the redevelopment. In 2009, a team led by Urban Splash, including architects Hawkins\Brown and Studio Egret West, began stripping the blocks back to their concrete shells and reconfiguring them, mainly as upmarket flats for upmarket brutalists.

Concrete Quarterly reported on the project in 2011, just as the first flats were going on the market. The most prominent aesthetic change was to the facades, which had originally been arranged in three-bay units: one of glazing and two of brick infill. Now the solid-to-void ratio had been swapped round, with two-bay windows drawing more daylight into the bedrooms. The third bay was a brightly coloured panel, part Le Corbusier, part Apple—indeed, they had been made from the same material as iPod cases. The suspended link bridges—an integral part of the streets-in-the-air approach—had been retained, although now there was to be concierge access. Meanwhile, an external mirror-finished helical stair and glazed external lift offered a more welcoming entrance to the development.

The changes had helped to reduce the "fortress-like impermeability" of the original design, Concrete Quarterly noted, but the scheme's success lay in working with the original concept with "a deference that is intelligent and well placed".[11] Perhaps encouraged by this, Mikhail Riches, the architect of the next phase of the regeneration, is adopting even more of a light touch, retaining the brickwork and taking inspiration from the traces of former residents, as well as the estate's graffiti. The redevelopment is scheduled for completion in 2022.

Olympic Aquatics Centre
London, UK
Zaha Hadid Architects, Arup

Issue 241, Autumn 2012

Above: The double-curved roof is supported at only three points—from the two cores and a supporting wall at the southern end.

Right: The 50-metre competition pool had to be cast extremely carefully in 10-metre by 10-metre bays to minimise cracking.

Left: The walls were made of self-compacting concrete and left exposed in all areas.

Above: The curved parts of the walls required specialist formwork manufactured from phenolic ply.

Not since the Festival of Britain had London made such a concerted effort to enjoy itself. The 2012 Olympics was a massive undertaking—a £6.8 billion project involving five new major sports venues, swaths of parkland, roads, bridges and housing, all in the name of sport. Surprisingly for the Olympics, the showpiece architectural statement was not the main stadium—which was to be partially deconstructed after the event—but the Aquatics Centre, designed by Zaha Hadid Architects. With its swirling roof flanked by enormous stands of temporary seating, *Concrete Quarterly* thought it looked like a "vast stingray gliding among the teeming thousands".[12]

The Aquatics Centre is the finest example in Britain of Zaha Hadid Architects' sheer verve when it came to using concrete. The material is structure, substructure and finish—and even turns diving boards into sinuous sculptures. Below ground, it is concrete at its most muscular: the complex site on former industrial land required 1,800 piles and 3-metre-thick bridging slabs over a network of buried power tunnels. But above ground it is all grace. The walls surrounding the competition pools dipped and swelled in concave and convex shapes, formed using a self-compacting mix to help it flow around the reinforcement. Though these walls sometimes gave the impression of being double-curved, this was in fact an illusion: "If you cut a diagonal slice from a cylinder it can look this way", explained Zaha Hadid Architects project architect Sara Klomps.

The beautiful coffered ceiling of the training pool, meanwhile, was poured in sections as a 1.2-metre-deep slab, but using special formers to create the petal-shaped lighting troughs. Even though the roof spans over 25 metres, the decreased weight of the coffered design, together with the use of high-strength concrete and 40–50 millimetre high-tensile bar reinforcement, made it immensely strong and self-supporting.

And then there were the diving boards, poised like cobras. These were cast in repeatable 2.5-metre-high sections using heavy-duty fibreglass moulds, and contained a surprisingly dense network of reinforcement. Although the boards needed to support only their own weight (and occasionally that of a diver), they cantilevered off the ground at an angle and had huge forces acting upon them. It took 462 tonnes of concrete but the result was an iconic sight of the Games—and surely one of the most beautiful pieces of sporting equipment ever created.

The four competition diving boards were cast in repeatable 2.5-metre-high sections using heavy-duty fibreglass moulds.

THE WORLD RECAST: 70 BUILDINGS FROM 70 YEARS OF *CONCRETE QUARTERLY*

The coffered ceiling of the training pool was poured as a 1.2-metre-deep slab, using special formers to create the petal-shaped troughs.

Stamp House
Queensland, Australia
Charles Wright Architects

Issue 246, Winter 2013

Above: A bridge connects the swampy
site to dry ground.

Right: 14-metre cantilevers keep
the living areas above the flood line
at all times.

Below: The central living area is left open to the elements.

Right: An irregular star-shaped roof structure adds drama to the living space.[13]

Sixty years after Richard Neutra placed exposed concrete at the heart of luxury living, a house in Far North Queensland took the material in a slightly different direction. Charles Wright Architects' Stamp House was a "third way between luxury holiday and survival weekend", wrote *Concrete Quarterly*—"the kind of place where a Bond villain or Vladimir Putin might choose to unwind".[13]

On the one hand, the holiday house had all of the sophistication one would expect of an exclusive getaway. At the heart of the building is an open courtyard with a pool. From here, six cantilevered wings radiated out, housing en-suite bedrooms and outdoor lounges. The finishes were minimalist and of the highest quality, with polished concrete floors, marble bathrooms and all services embedded seamlessly into the slab and walls (some of these elements were precast and some cast in situ).

On the other hand, the structure also had "the strength and self-sufficiency of a high-grade military bunker". The Stamp House is situated in the middle of Queensland's rainforest, an area prone to extreme weather in the wet season. In response, Wright effectively designed a deluxe cyclone shelter—which came in handy when the category 5 Cyclone Yasi struck midway through construction.

From the walls of the 14-metre cantilevers to the irregular star-shaped 'waffle' ceiling above the central area, the reinforced concrete structure was immense. "The walls to each wing are actually the structural beams that support the entire building, so they're incredibly thick—an average of 650–700

millimetres", said Wright. In order to support such a heavy structure, more than 30 piles had to be driven 12 metres down into the swampy site.

Because of the remoteness of the house, it also had to be capable of sustaining itself if cut off by bad weather. The roof was covered in solar panels, which had a two-month storage capacity, eliminating the need for a backup fossil-fuel generator. And there was a vast concrete tank beneath the pool that harvests up to 250,000 litres of rainwater—enough to fill 1,000 bathtubs.

One slightly quirky feature was the decoration on the facade. The client was a stamp dealer and, to reflect this, the exterior was given perforations like the edges of a stamp. The effect was simply achieved: "We screw-fixed the PVC caps from some piping to the formwork", said Wright. "It was quite crude but it yielded the result we wanted."

If the philately theme rather undermined the super-cool Bond villain vibe, Wright assured that the facade would soon gain a suitable air of mystery. "In the tropics, concrete develops a dark stain, or patina. This will become part of the house's character—the idea is that it will grow into the jungle."

Everyman Theatre
Liverpool, UK
Haworth Tompkins,
Alan Baxter & Associates

Issue 248, Summer 2014

Above: The facade includes 100 panels etched with the portraits of Liverpool residents.

Right: Frederick Gibberd's Metropolitan Cathedral looms over the theatre.

Opposite: The combination of exposed concrete and brickwork provides excellent thermal mass, allowing the auditorium to be naturally ventilated.

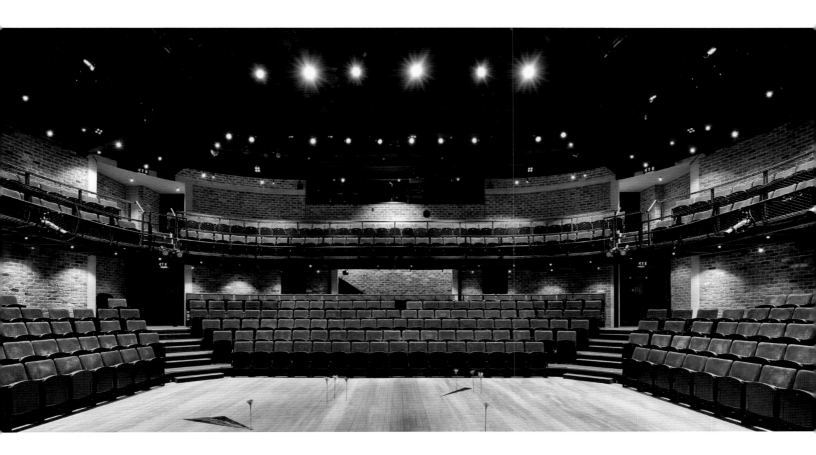

Radical theatre first collided with concrete architecture in the 1960s. The spirit of the times demanded a new design language, and Coventry, Nottingham and Chichester were all given bold, brutalist playhouses deemed ideal for staging new works that were both publicly funded and, more often than not, pitted against the system. By 2014, however, the tear-it-down spirit of the 1960s had given way to a more polite attitude to heritage. Nottingham and Chichester had both been restored and sensitively updated—now respectable citizens rather than angry young men.

The task facing Haworth Tompkins at Liverpool's Everyman was somewhat harder. The Everyman was not one of the 1960s' brave new playhouses. Founded in 1964, it was initially accommodated in a small nineteenth-century chapel before being completely rebuilt in 1977. This new building was almost as cramped and "primitive in the extreme".[14] What it did have was a tremendous atmosphere. Throughout the 1960s and 70s it gained a nationwide reputation for groundbreaking theatre but was also legendary for its front-of-house. As its name suggests, it saw itself as a place for the people, where audiences could mix with actors, poets and writers in a heady ambiance of conviviality and creativity.

So Haworth Tompkins needed to keep nothing and everything of the old building. While the facilities needed to be completely remodelled, and the theatre was to announce itself as a new civic presence in Liverpool, they somehow had to retain the essence of the Everyman of legend. Will Mesher, an associate at the firm, explained how, as the ethos of the institution was always very informal and friendly,

we didn't want to make it more intimidating or upmarket. The use of natural and self-finished materials, rather than more polished finishes, was part of that.[15]

The trick was to temper this informal, industrial aesthetic with a sense of civic scale. Mesher pointed out that, as one of only a few big civic institutions in Liverpool—and one that occupied a historic site next to Frederick Gibberd's Metropolitan Cathedral—the theatre had to look refined rather than rough and ready. The interiors resonated with copper and steel mesh, offset by meticulously detailed, board-marked in-situ concrete walls and columns. To get the best possible finish from the 75-millimetre softwood boards, extensive tests were carried out on 1-metre cubed samples, while equal care was taken over the concrete's colour. A tone that was both warm and fairly pale was achieved by replacing about one-third of the cement with ground granulated blast furnace slag (GGBS).

The use of GGBS, which is a by-product of the iron-making industry, was in keeping with the whole ethos of the development. New materials were used sparingly, and the brickwork and roof timbers were all salvaged from the previous theatre. The theme of continuity that had driven the project had segued neatly into sustainability. For an urban theatre, with its complex lighting and heating demands, this was an impressively low-energy operation. The swaths of exposed concrete provided thermal mass to control temperature, and natural ventilation was used for all the main performance and workspaces. Theatre design in the twenty-first century still had something important to say; it just preferred not to shout about it.

Top: The theatre occupies a prominent site between the Anglican and Roman Catholic cathedrals.

Above: Throughout the building, black steel and timber provide a contrast to the exposed concrete.

Right: The open front-of-house area maintains the theatre's informal, friendly atmosphere.

Right: Ground granulated blast furnace slag was used as a cement replacement to create a warm, fairly pale finish to the concrete.

Below: The material palette also includes bricks reclaimed from the previous theatre building.

2010–2017

Burntwood School
London, UK
Allford Hall Monaghan Morris,
Buro Happold

Issue 253, Autumn 2015

Above: The AHMM scheme includes
four four-storey teaching pavilions,
a sports hall and a performing arts
centre amid existing buildings
designed by Leslie Martin.

Right: The architects used just
15 different panel types to create
the sculpted effect of the precast
concrete facades.

The base panels are of acid-etched black concrete, while the upper panels use a pale cement and quartz-like aggregate.

Burntwood School was the last hurrah of a government programme that lavished billions of pounds on new school buildings, then ground to a halt amid public-spending cuts and global economic gloom. The irony of Allford Hall Monaghan Morris (AHMM)'s design was that there was nothing profligate about it. By reminding schools that repetitive, precast elements in inexpensive, robust materials could be beautiful, it actually pointed a way forward.

Over the past two decades, AHMM has helped to establish concrete as a desirable, not to say pragmatic, aesthetic for new British schools. To many headteachers in the early 2000s, concrete was indelibly linked with school estates from the 1960s that they deemed outdated and unfit-for-purpose. In a 2016 interview, Paul Monaghan, AHMM's co-founder, quoted one: "I don't care what it is, I like everything... apart from concrete."[16]

This began to change with AHMM's Westminster Academy in London, which was shortlisted for the 2008 Stirling Prize. The practice showed how a raw finish could be brought to boisterous life with a sky of coloured acoustic baffles, bold graphics (by long-time collaborator Morag Myerscough) and inventive use of filtered lighting. It was spectacular, robust and inexpensive: "We had very simple plywood boarding that we'd use three times to save money", Monaghan recalled. "We weren't that bothered about the lines."

If Westminster Academy had challenged perceptions about concrete schools, there was still one taboo: precast. As Monaghan put it: "Unless you're in a really sophisticated world, the two words 'prefabricated concrete' don't really work with clients." At Dagenham Park School, he set out to show that the repetition inherent in precast construction could, with subtle variation, be a thing of beauty in itself. AHMM varied the rhythm by using bright red and orange solar control fins, and added depth and shade with a pronounced picture frame around each window. Monaghan won the headteacher round with photographs of "total repetition"—in the form of the Georgian terraces of Bedford Square in central London.

Which brings us to Burntwood, the 2015 Stirling Prize winner. As with Dagenham Park, the beauty of the elevations stemmed directly from the controlled variation of repeated elements. Now though, the use of relief and expression went far beyond the window frames—in fact, it defined the whole facade. The sculpted effect was created using a palette of just 15 different precast moulds, and, because the panels were self-supporting, they could be thicker than at Dagenham Park, accentuating the sense of depth. The other variation was the use of two mixes: the base panels were acid-etched black concrete with flecks of mica, while the upper panels, also acid-etched, used an off-white cement with a dark quartz-like aggregate.

Throughout the school, small details show the lessons gleaned from two decades of experimentation: there are the raw interiors and Myerscough graphics; there's the 'corduroy' pattern of precast concrete that gives a strong line to the base of the building, despite the changing ground level; and the subtly different treatments of the two floors of the sports hall, one using polished, the other honed black precast panels.

It was always likely that Burntwood School would be built in concrete. The existing 1950s buildings on the site were designed by leading modernist Leslie Martin, the co-designer of the Royal Festival Hall, and the senior education team quickly revealed themselves to be ardent modern architecture fans. AHMM's design was clearly influenced by Marcel Breuer's precast facades—Flaine ski resort in the Alps or the IBM Building in Boca Raton, Florida—with their robust, faceted panels. But whereas Breuer rather enjoyed the cold, hard factory finishes of the machine age, Burntwood was more richly coloured and softer edged, its deep hollows like drifts of sand. It would take a headteacher with a heart of reconstituted stone not to fall for it.

Left: The depth of the sculpted panels also helps to screen classrooms from the sun.

Below: A combination of polished and honed black precast concrete panels are used on the sports hall.

Opposite: The use of geometric tiles around the entrances adds an element of colour.

Blavatnik School of Government
Oxford, UK
Herzog & de Meuron,
Pell Frischmann

Issue 256, Summer 2016

Above: "This building is winding itself up"—the concrete slabs spiral around a central atrium.

Right: The building rises in a stack of glazed volumes, each a different shape.

Left: The floor slabs cantilever over the central space by up to 9 metres.

Below: The spiral staircase at the back of the building was precast on site then lowered into the enclosed cylindrical structure.

Faced with the beauty of Oxford's historic buildings, argued Jacques Herzog at the unveiling of the Blavatnik School of Government, most modernist architects "tried to be modern but nevertheless behave well. And it's very difficult to behave well and do it the right way without losing your own identity."[17] Herzog & de Meuron's building is a fascinating response to this quandary. In some ways it is the most alien building ever to land on Oxford, but it is also engaged in active conversation with both the city's classical heritage and the modernist response to that heritage.

On a prominent site directly opposite the neoclassical Oxford University Press, the School of Government rises as a stack of five glass drums framed in bands of concrete. These drums are all of different shapes, creating a series of overhangs, setbacks and terraces. Only the rotunda-like top two floors stack neatly on top of one another. Inside, an atrium spirals up the full height of the building, shifting at each level with the irregular plan. The floorplates, wrapped in concrete balustrades, seem to float above the forum, thanks to cantilevers up to 9 metres deep. Coupled with the swooping staircases down to the basement and up to the first floor, as well as a separate in-situ concrete spiral staircase at the back of the forum, the effect is of unspooling tape. "The building is winding itself up", Herzog explained, "so it offers views and perspectives in all directions. People can be on these balconies and overlook this central space, or talk from different levels."

The materials were both resonant of their context and defiantly modern: oak panelling was used in playful riposte to the university's fusty senior common rooms; glazing was generous (including the largest single plate of glass in Europe); and the in-situ concrete walls, soffits and stairs were all the honeyish colour of the local limestone. Genuine limestone would have been the obvious choice in Oxford, but Herzog & de Meuron partner Ascan Mergenthaler told *Concrete Quarterly*, "it would be almost like a cliché. It was important we used today's building materials."

All of the concrete was cast in situ, using the practice's characteristic approach. The historian Adrian Forty has noted how architects such as Peter Zumthor, Peter Märkli and Herzog & de Meuron, all schooled at the Eidgenössische Technische Hochschule in Zurich in the 1960s and 70s, "exploit concrete's sensuous and tactile properties, and its capacity to suggest that buildings were 'real', the outcome of an actual process of construction".[18] The result is a relaxedness about the occasional imperfection in the finished concrete: what you strike is what you get.

Of course, this places a greater onus on specifying the correct mix in the first place. "We did a lot of mock-ups to get the right mix, the right tone, the right methods, and so on", said Mergenthaler. The team eventually decided on a high-flow concrete with 40 per cent of the cement replaced by ground granulated blast furnace slag. This lightened the colour, drawing out the tone of the locally sourced limestone aggregate.

One of the major challenges of the build was the inherent instability of the 'floating' structure. It was important that the floor slabs looked delicate, but at just 300 millimetres thick they couldn't support the deep cantilevers that define both the internal and external form of the building. Pell Frischmann's structural design solved this by using the walls above the slabs as cantilever beams. The whole thing was then held together by the fourth floor—a 350-millimetre-thick slab that was post-tensioned to give it sufficient tensile strength to span the atrium.

It may all sound slightly extravagant, but the School of Government actually included a number of respectful nods to its rarefied surroundings. The rectilinear first-floor facade is a deliberate continuation of the line of the portico of the Greek Revival church next door, and the building tactfully steps back from the main road as it rises. The spiralling atrium, meanwhile, was a reference to the city's cold, windswept quadrangles: "You are shocked when you see the beauty of these colleges; they have these open courtyards which we couldn't do, as the programme was so big and the site was very small", Herzog explained. "But that impulse to make a central space was here at the very beginning."

The dreaming spires of Oxford had greeted many new concrete neighbours in the twentieth century, particularly in the 1960s and 70s. Now they had a dreaming spiral.

2010–2017

Stavros Niarchos Foundation Cultural Centre
Athens, Greece
Renzo Piano Building Workshop, Expedition

Issue 260, Summer 2017

Above: The canopy comprises 717
prefabricated panels, and is believed
to be the largest ferrocement span in
the world.

Opposite: The roof shelters a terrace
and glass-walled library.

Concrete structures have often signified defiance. In the post-war period, rebuilding in such a solid, unyielding material was a statement of permanence, the first manifestations of a brighter future. And the bigger, higher or stronger the structure, the more emphatic the statement. There is a sense of this defiance with the Stavros Niarchos Foundation Cultural Centre (SNFCC) in Athens, designed by Renzo Piano Building Workshop. With the Greek cultural ministry's budget now less than half what it was when the project was planned in 2007, the €600 million centre has been funded entirely by the eponymous late shipping magnate's foundation. But it is a powerful civic gesture, expressed loudly and clearly by a groundbreaking concrete structure.

The landmark flourish of the 22,000-square-metre building is a canopy that stretches 100 metres in both directions to shelter a vast terrace with views over both city and sea. This is believed to be the largest span ever made from ferrocement—the mesh and mortar-based material that Pier Luigi Nervi had used to build the Turin Exhibition Hall. Like Nervi, Piano has previously built a yacht from the material, but the SNFCC, which will house the Greek National Opera and Greek National Library within a new public park, is on another scale.

The main building structure has a conventional reinforced concrete frame, incorporating large expanses of fair-faced concrete and a number of long-span transfer structures over atriums and auditoriums. For the canopy, the initial plan was to use a lighter, steel-framed structure but it became clear that this couldn't deliver Piano's desired aesthetic. "It was very important that it should be visually very light and fine and with a completely un-jointed bottom surface", Bruce Martin of UK structural engineer Expedition told Concrete Quarterly. "We saw that ferrocement had the potential to deliver the finish, and form curved profiles, to a very high quality."[19]

The canopy has clear internal spans of up to 75 metres, cantilevers 12.5 metres at the front and tapers in depth from 4.4 metres to just 23 centimetres at its edge. It is formed from two load-bearing 'skins' linked by tubular steel bracing that carries shear forces. Each ferrocement skin was created using up to six layers of fine-diameter steel mesh encased in a cement mortar. Almost all of the 717 prefabricated panels were unique, to take into account variations in curvature. Mindful of the possibility of variations in the colour of the white mortar over the expanse of the canopy underside, the design team opted to paint the finished surface.

Piano and Expedition's "floating" roof prompted a lively debate at Concrete Quarterly about whether or not it should grace the cover of the Summer 2017 issue. "The crux of the matter was this", explained The Concrete Centre's Guy Thompson in his leader column, "did the image need to look obviously 'concretey'?"[20]

The SNFCC made the cover. In 2017, it seems concrete doesn't have to look like concrete. In any case, as Thompson pointed out, "What exactly does that mean, when concrete can assume such diverse forms?"

1   Bizley, Graham, "Hadid Makes History", *Concrete Quarterly*, Issue 230, Winter 2009, pp 6–9.

2   "Ponti", *Concrete Quarterly*, Issue 91, Winter 1971, p 24.

3   "Floating Fortress", *Concrete Quarterly*, Issue 237, Autumn 2011, pp 10–11.

4   Pearson, Andy, "Ripples of Delight", *Concrete Quarterly*, Issue 253, Autumn 2015, p 7.

5   "Pier Luigi Nervi", *Concrete Quarterly*, Issue 25, Summer 1955, p 28.

6   "The Sainsbury Laboratory – RIBA Stirling Prize Winner 2012", video, 4 min 2 sec, last modified 17 October 2012, www.vimeo.com/51603839.

7   "Research Lab Takes Root", *Concrete Quarterly*, Issue 233, Autumn 2010, pp 12–13.

8   Stanton, Alan, "Lasting Impression", *Concrete Quarterly*, Issue 248, 2014, p.19. All subsequent quotations in this section are from the same article.

9   Smith, Ivor, lecture given for the centenary celebrations of the School of Architecture at the University of Sheffield, 15 April 2008.

10 Sillitoe, David, "The Utopian Estate That's Been Left to Die", *The Guardian*, 5 March 2014, www.theguardian.com/artanddesign/the-camera-eye/2014/mar/05/park-hill-sheffield-utopian-estate-left-to-die.

11 "Return of the High Street", *Concrete Quarterly*, Issue 238, Winter 2011, pp 10–11.

12 Whitehead, Tony, "Whirl Pool", *Concrete Quarterly*, Issue 241, Autumn 2012, pp 4–7. All subsequent quotations in this section are from the same article.

13 "Collector's Item", *Concrete Quarterly*, Issue 246, Winter 2013, p 9. All subsequent quotations in this section are from the same article.

14 Hatton, Brian, "Everyman Theatre in Liverpool by Haworth Tompkins critiqued", *Architectural Review*, 16 October 2014, www.architectural-review.com/today/stirling-prize-winner-everyman-theatre-in-liverpool-by-haworth-tompkins-critiqued/8663364.article.

15 "Dramatic Entrance", *Concrete Quarterly*, Issue 248, Summer 2014, p 11. All subsequent quotations in this section are from the same article.

16 "The Road to Burntwood", *Concrete Quarterly*, Issue 253, Autumn 2015, pp 12–15. All subsequent quotations in this section are from the same article.

17 "Dreaming Spiral", *Concrete Quarterly*, Issue 256, Summer 2016, pp 4–7. All subsequent quotations in this section are from the same article.

18 Forty, Adrian, *Concrete and Culture: A Material History*, London: Reaktion Books, 2012, p 281.

19 Buxton, Pamela, "Piano's Lid", *Concrete Quarterly*, Issue 260, Summer 2017, pp 8–9.

20 Thompson, Guy, "Take the Advice of a 70-year-old…", *Concrete Quarterly*, Issue 260, Summer 2017, p 2. All subsequent quotations in this section are from the same article.

Featured Issues